LIFE GLEANINGS FROM REBBETZIN ROCHIE'S KITCHEN

The
RISING
LIFE

Challah Baking, Elevated.

ROCHIE PINSON

Published by ORLY PRESS
48 Cranford Place
Teaneck, NJ 07666

www.therisinglife.net

ORLY PRESS books may be purchased for educational, business or sales promotional use. For information please visit therisinglife.net.

Cover and book design: RP Design and Development
Cover photography: Saul Sudin
Illustrations: Lucy Engelman

pb ISBN 978-0-9890072-1-4

Pinson, Rochie 1975-
The Rising Life: Challah Baking, Elevated.
1.Judaism 2. Spirituality 3. Food

ORLY PRESS

ב״ה

THE
RISING
LIFE

CHALLAH BAKING. ELEVATED.

Life Gleanings from
Rebbetzin Rochie's Kitchen

This book is extracted from the cookbook
RISING! The Book of Challah

Feldheim Publishers 2015

My heart is full of gratitude.

For those who have nurtured me generously, and for those who have generously allowed me to nurture them.

For the incredible women who have inspired me throughout the writing of this book.

And for the women who made this book possible; Hillary Barr, Marilyn Brill, and Susan Polis-Schutz. I am eternally grateful for your presence and for your support.

CONTENTS

"ו‏היה באכלכם מלחם הארץ תרימו תרומה לה'....
ראשית ערסתכם חלה תרימו
תרומה כתרומת גרן כן תרימו אתה".

"The first of your dough, challah,
you shall offer as a gift. . . ."
— Bamidbar 15:19-20

"Reishit Arisoteichem"
The First of Your Dough
—

The word *reishit* indicates that which is the first, the finest, and the purpose of all that follows it. The removal and sanctification of the first and best of our dough illustrates a great truth of existence. That is, that all we do in this world, however mundane and ordinary it may seem, should begin with an acknowledgment of the Creator and a Higher Existence.

We begin every endeavor with the proclamation that *"l'Hashem ha'aretz um'loah/*The earth is G-d's and all that fills it" *(Tehillim 24:1)*.

The first and best of all that we accomplish is dedicated to a higher purpose.

We awaken in the morning and, with our first breath, sing praise to our Creator for the new day. Those less fortunate are fed before we take our own portion. We do not wait until we have finished with the "necessities" of life to get around to the "holiness."

"Reishit arisoteichem" is *"challah, l'Hashem."* The first and best of our sustenance is designated as challah for *Hashem/*G-d, and, as such, is dedicated to a higher purpose.

This is our truest reason for existence: to elevate and transcend through the work of our hands. Through making challah and separating the dough, we are perpetually bringing this awareness into our homes and into our lives.

May we merit to live a life in which we vividly observe the Divine unifying light in all of creation.

—

Taken from the words of the Lubavitcher Rebbe,
Rabbi Menachem M. Schneerson, OBM,
in his address to women, 17 Sivan, 5740/June 1, 1980.

RISING

Introduction
Challah as a Recipe for Life

RISING

This book is not a cookbook.

Don't get me wrong; by the time you've finished reading this book, and its sister book, *RISING!*, you'll have learned how to bake challah, gained tried-and-true tips on things like freezing, storing, and serving, as well as added a plethora of challah recipes to your repertoire.

So, why isn't this a cookbook? Well, for one, I'm not a professionally trained chef or baker (I do put out a three-course meal twice weekly—but that's just because I'm a rebbetzin and when each Friday rolls around, it's time to cook lots of food for lots of guests—whether or not I've ever actually learned to cook . . . more on that later).

And secondly, these books set out to be substantially more than just a collection of recipes, directions, and really pretty pictures (although I've put in lots of those, too. I like a pretty picture as much as the next girl).

So, what is this book?

This is a book for those of us who find ourselves wishing for a return to a simpler time, a slower pace, a scent of bread baking in the home, and a sense of peace in the moment. This little book wants to be that big alarm on the iPhone of our subconscious that reminds us that the mess in our kitchen, the noise in our brain, the stickiness of the dough underneath our fingernails, and the aroma of warm challah on a cold Friday afternoon means that we are not merely alive, we are living, and that that is a wonderful thing.

A challah dough is a living organism. It requires air, water, attention, and intention. Its recipe so closely mirrors the recipe for a well-balanced life, in fact, that as I baked my challah each week, I kept learning new things about the care and attention required by the living beings under my watch (children, husband, community, and the like), and thus, *RISING*, the blog, and eventually, the book and the cookbook, were born.

The Rising Life, as the first part in the *RISING* series, is a book that sets out to explore what happens when we decide to put ourselves wholly into the nurturing process, recognizing that the physical care and feeding of ourselves and those we love is only one side of a sticky dough. Fold it over and you will find that there is a whole other side that hasn't been worked on yet. (See, I'm starting with the challah metaphors already!)

The Perfect Challah

So, disclaimer disclaimed, I am not a professional chef, nor am I a baker. I'm not even a licensed expert in child raising, whatever that may be. But here's what I've learned over my years of challah baking and child raising: we don't need to earn a PhD in child psychology before becoming parents (even if we did, it wouldn't necessarily be helpful!), we don't need to be a licensed therapist to offer a comforting hug and listening ear to a friend, and, likewise, we don't need to go through culinary school to bake the perfect challah.

The perfect challah is one that is baked with intention and love and served in much the same way. The perfect challah is like the perfect nurturer. Psychoanalyst Donald Winnicott, observer of thousands of mothers in their nurturing roles, coined the term "the good enough mother" and recognized that the "perfect nurturer" is not perfect at all; she is human and very real indeed.

The "good enough mother" gets back up when she falls down, provides for her loved ones both physically and emotionally (and, I add, spiritually), and is genuinely preoccupied with her nurturing role. The "good enough mother" is more of a gardener than a goddess.

The "good enough mother" recognizes that just like challah dough, we grow in cycles. Each cycle offers a new opportunity to learn the same things. The very same lessons will come up toward us time and again. The seasons change, the children grow, and we ourselves mature. When we understand our role in parenting and nurturing in this way, we can forgive ourselves and take the pressure off of ourselves to get it right the very first time.

The perfect mother recognizes that to give of the very best of herself is as close as to perfection as she can get.

And therein lies the secret to the perfect challah:

It's not a perfect challah at all.

It's a "good enough challah." It's your challah. It is not so much about the end result, it is about what happens during the process. When the process of making challah is one of intention and presence, the challah that is formed will rise and be delicious. It may not look like it came out of a bakery, but that's not the point. We are looking to create something that comes from us and is unique to who we are.

The Perfect Nurturer

When we nurture, we need to do so from the deepest part of ourselves; trying to fit into a "cookie-cutter" mold of nurturing will only frustrate and be harmful to both ourselves and our loved ones, cheating them of our full nurturing potential. To nurture is to be aware of our most true self and to give from that place.

All of our actions and behaviors are derivatives of the emotional energy and intention that drive those actions. And they are usually received the same way they have been directed. Ever heard the expressions, "feeling the love on the plate" or, conversely, "eating humble pie"? We can sense in a deep way when the food that has been prepared for us has been done so lovingly and with intention, just as well as we can tell when there is anger or resentment in the food that is placed before us. When we feed our loved ones, the food they receive is absorbed and transferred into actual energy. The love and intention we put into our food preparation informs the energy that will be created from that food! We make challah from a place of commitment to nourish ourselves and our families in a way that goes beyond mere physical feeding and watering.

RISING

There will be days when we feel fully risen and expansive and up to facing life's most difficult challenges, and we will gaze at our lovely fat challahs with pride. There will also be days when we may feel deeply deflated and incapable, and the slightly lopsided challah cooling on the counter may be reflective of that state of mind. Through all the risings and the fallings, though, the knowledge that we are good enough to nurture, exactly as we are, will help us appreciate the yield of our efforts, and recognize the loveliness in all its yummy imperfection.

My Journey With Challah

So, how does this self-described "imperfect-but-trying-really-hard" mom end up writing a book on challah?

I kind of figured out this challah thing on my own. My mother had an unfortunate experience with a challah dough in the early days of her marriage and didn't try again. It was strictly bakery-made challah for us from then on.[1] Not having grown up in a challah-baking household, I always marveled at the homes I entered on Friday that smelled like baking challah. In my mind, this was the perfect smell for a home that was about to welcome Shabbat.

---

1 As of this writing, I am thrilled to say that my mother has been inspired and encouraged by my challah baking and has since started making her very own challah after 40 years of marriage. Of course, it goes without saying that she uses the classic recipe from this book (see page 173) and her challah rivals mine most weeks. I am truly delighted and share this fact with all my challah workshop students as it demonstrates that it is never too late to learn to make challah or, for that matter, to master anything that frightens us.

When I married and started my own Shabbat traditions, I knew that a home that smelled of baking challah needed to be part of my new life. The question was . . . how?

Well, the answer came in the form of an emergency . . . as many answers tend to come to me. Note: I work best under intense pressure!

Young and newly married to a rabbi, I had excitedly accepted the offer to travel with my husband to Kobe, Japan for the High Holidays to bring some inspiration and Torah to the small community still remaining there.

The detail they neglected to mention, (maybe because it was obvious to all but myself,) was that as the "rebbetzin in residence," I was assumed to be a chef, or at least fairly proficient in the kitchen. Maybe this was to be expected, but I was young and naïve (come to think of it, I'm thankfully still pretty naïve – just a little less young) and had let others do the cooking for me for most of my life.

Arriving in Kobe, I was informed that the community was eagerly awaiting my delicious Rosh Hashanah meals . . . insert slight panic mode here. Following multiple frantic (and expensive!) transatlantic calls to my dear mother back in Canada, I managed to figure out how to make the basic foods for the holiday. And then, in all my sweet innocence, I asked our host whether he wanted me to go and buy the challah for the holiday or had been planning to go himself. Needless to say, he found my question very amusing and informed me in a good-natured way (that still sounded very intimidating to this young newlywed) that, of course, the rebbetzin would bake the challah for the community. There is no kosher bakery in Kobe, apparently.

RISING

The slight panic turned into very real panic now, as Rosh Hashanah was to begin the following evening and if there was one thing I did not feel qualified to do, it was to bake challah, let alone for some 200 people. Cue the frantic, expensive, transatlantic calls once more and, this time, my mother was panicking right along with me—she had never (successfully) baked challah, either! So, my mother read the recipe to me and I faithfully copied it down (this was pre-send-a-photo-of-the-recipe-by-text days) and got to work.

Many hours later, I was dusted in a coating of flour. A veritable human schnitzel, sticky pieces of dough had lodged themselves into my hair and up my arms. My back was aching from all the rolling and kneading, I was exhausted and exhilarated . . . and there were 40 somewhat misshapen but fantastic-smelling challahs lined up on the counter of an unfamiliar kitchen. What can I say? It may not sound like much fun to you, but I was hooked.

When I served that challah on Rosh Hashanah, it truly felt like a new beginning. I had done something I hadn't thought I could ever do and opened the door to the possibility that I could pretty much do anything I set my mind toward.

I came back home to the shores of "Jew York," where kosher bakeries are plentiful and the need to bake my own challah was not nearly as urgent, but was determined to find a way to make challah baking a part of my new home and life.

Full disclosure: the first week's challahs weren't that great. Neither were the second. As mentioned, I work better under (intense) pressure and, somehow, the call to bake challah for just myself and my husband didn't work as well on me as the nearly impossible task of making five batches of challah on my very first try. But I was determined and persevered.

As the weeks went on, my challah baking became more streamlined. I worked it neatly (more or less—my husband may perhaps argue that it was not so neat—I still make a royal mess every time I bake challah) into my Friday routine and it became the one Shabbat food I and my family wouldn't do without.

And something incredible happened. As I kneaded my way through numerous moves (and their accompanying kitchens), pregnancies, childbirths, sleepless nights, job changes, illness and loss, my challah baking became something more—exponentially more—than the act of baking bread.

Each week, as I mixed the ingredients into my large, by now well-used, stainless steel challah bowl, scooped up the flour stuck to the bottom, kneaded and pounded and massaged, I began to feel the challah dough echoing the sounds (and, at times, cacophony) of my life. The act of making the challah, the mitzvah of taking the small piece of dough with the blessing, and the rolling and braiding of the strands, became meditative, meaningful, therapeutic, and soul-refreshing.

It occurred to me one week, in the deep humidity of August, that the stickiness of a dough that just wouldn't become "perfect" would still end up as delicious challah. I then realized that if I only put my love and care into the sticky situation I was currently dealing with in my life, things would turn out pretty okay, as well.

While scooping up some leftover dried bits of flour that didn't seem to want to become part of the whole and incorporating them gently into my growing dough, I found that, soon enough, they seamlessly joined. Maybe the people who viewed themselves as outsiders would, in our efforts to reach out and gently include them, feel loved and part of something bigger and beautiful.

Each ingredient became significant, each act in the process of creating and braiding and baking the dough became infused with meaning, and I realized that the challah baking was growing into something bigger. It was rising.

I found myself running to my computer each week after placing the challah dough in its bowl to rise, and jotting down my thoughts, experiences, and epiphanies of that week's challah baking.

In my capacity as rebbetzin of a quickly growing community, I began to find that as I spoke with women about their hopes, frustrations, sorrows, and triumphs, challah baking was somehow always there to guide me in its wisdom. I began teaching a monthly challah class, drawing in women from all walks of life; somehow challah baking was calling out to women everywhere—people we had met and hadn't heard from in years were suddenly asking to be included in the next challah class. I had to close registration on each class and open waiting lists that stretched into the following year.

I was on to something.

Challah baking awakened something in women, a deeply rooted feminine desire to nurture—and nurture creatively and positively—that we had perhaps ignored for a long time. There was something in the challah baking that spoke to us as women, as builders and listeners, that called out to be answered.

And how the women have answered! Over the past decade of challah classes taught all over the world, I have received emails, letters, and calls from around the globe that testify to the incredible power of challah baking and how it is so much more than meets the eye.

Throughout this book I invite you into my little kitchen as we mix, measure, knead, and shape, and open up to the possibilities that baking challah can bring into your life. It is my hope and prayer that the ancient wisdom in challah that has guided me in my own journey will do the same for you, dear reader, and give rise to a happier home and a more confident, nurturing you.

"THE GREATEST GIFT IS A PORTION OF THYSELF."

—RALPH WALDO EMERSON

Chapter I
The Gift of Challah

*"The first of your dough, **challah**, you shall offer as a gift . . . ."*
—*Bamidbar 15:20*

". . . and it shall be a gift for all generations."
—*Bamidbar 15:21*

I used to think that if I gave something away, I would have less.

Indeed, in a universe dictated by the laws of physics, this seems to be the case. When we give away a portion of our money, a smaller sum remains. When we take time out of our day to do something for another, we end up with less time to allot for other purposes.

A verse in the Torah counters this belief and tells us that the more we give away, the more we will, in fact, have.

The words *"Asser te'asser/*You shall surely tithe" *(Bamidbar 14:22)*, can also be read as *"Asser **te'asher**,"* changing the translation to "Tithe and you will be wealthy." Our sages interpret this phrase to mean "Through the giving of your wealth you will become wealthy" *(Taanit 9a)*.

Kind of turns our thinking on its head.

Challah, as a practice and a privilege, has been given to us to prove this theory.

Giving is Receiving

Nurturing others in the "me" generation has become increasingly and singularly difficult. We have been raised to believe that we need to always take excellent care of ourselves, cultivate our wants and desires, and consistently make sure we are putting ourselves first.

This has benefited humanity in many ways, primarily in that it has allowed women to voice their true tendencies and desires and step forward into multitudes of new possibilities, giving the world strong female leaders. Yet, conversely, it seems to have made all forms of nurturing, especially parenting, all the more difficult and conflicted.

Having gotten used to feeling that we must put ourselves first, putting another life ahead of our own and answering another's wants and desires before our own seems counterintuitive and possibly damaging to ourselves. Surrounded by need, in all its many incarnations, we feel cheated of our "me" time and struggle with the sensation that something has been taken away from us.

In those early days of child raising and learning to be a MOTHER (yes, capitals on that one), I struggled mightily with the feeling that my creativity, that very thing that fueled me, was being trampled upon. Thinking about my next shower seemed just about as much as I could handle, never mind having a whole lucid thought, let alone an idea. Who was I?

I kept hearing this phrase from experienced parents (accompanied by the requisite sagely head–nod), "Long days, short years." I didn't get it then. If the days felt so endlessly long, just imagine the years!

But, as the days slowly, slowly, went by, I started to experience bursts of pure joy that broke me open with their sharp edges of clarity. And, shockingly, as desperately as I desired my space and my "me" time, these jolts of joy were occurring in my moments of pure dedication to this new life.

Ironic. When we give of ourselves in a way that is true to who we are, we receive so much more than we give. We exit fuller than we entered. Just like flames, we give light to others and become brighter in the process.

This is challah.

Connecting to Perfection

Challah is a *mitzvah*.

Mitzvah is often translated as commandment, although it also stems from the word *tzavta*/connection. At its essence, a mitzvah is a connector. It is an opportunity through which we can connect with our deepest selves and with our Creator.

As the Jewish nation stood on the threshold of a new reality, at the borders of the land they would soon conquer, cultivate, and love forever, they received a plethora of instructions. Each of these served as an opportunity through which to remain connected while farming, harvesting, baking, and living. Of these mitzvot, one stands out as particularly powerful, connective, and eternal: the mitzvah of challah.

"And it shall be when you eat from the bread of the land, you shall offer up a gift for G-d. The first of your dough, challah, you shall offer as a gift . . ." (Bamidbar 15:19-20). Verse 21 continues by stating that this will be a gift for future generations, as well.

We start with a seemingly perfect ball of dough, beautifully round, having combined the basic ingredients of life—water, air, and matter—to create something more than the sum of its parts. Yet, we are told, this dough is not complete. It is not yet whole. We must remove a piece of this dough to create perfection.

The Balancing Act

So here's where the idea of challah started to really connect for me. At the age of 34, I was diagnosed with a serious illness. At an age where mortality was not something I had ever considered, and the invincibility of my 20s had not quite worn off, I was told that I had a potentially fatal disease. The prognosis was excellent and I am, thank G-d, alive and well to tell the tale, but the treatment involved removing a part of me that I had never given much thought to before, yet suddenly took on tremendous importance. Having never gone through surgery or illness, it seemed to me that this removal of a piece of myself would render me incomplete, somehow less than I had been before.

That Friday morning, one day after having received my diagnosis and a few days before Yom Kippur, the most awe-inspiring day of reckoning, a day when we mimic death to feel the shock of mortality, I found myself elbow-deep in my challah dough, as always. But, this time it was different. I was kneading and hoping and praying—and, as always, finding more of myself in the process—when it occurred to me that the challah, so perfect looking and whole, was, in fact, incomplete. It required the removal of that little piece of dough to attain its fullness. "Ahhh," I thought, "this is what it's about." We give and give of ourselves and think that it is depleting us, but, truthfully, it is precisely through the giving of ourselves that we become more whole.

As I went through my illness and all its consequential sufferings in the quest for healing, I kept hearing over and over, "It's time to take care of yourself now." To tell the truth, I had been so busy taking care of my babies, my husband, my community, and my career as a graphic designer, I wasn't actually sure what taking care of myself even looked like. In fact, though I felt happy and fulfilled, there was a part of me that felt markedly depleted.

Thus began my search for a balance in the care for myself and nurturing of others. I will not say that I've figured it out completely, except to say that I've figured out that it's a lifelong balancing act, one that requires constant checking and re-calibration. And, in my challah-baking practice, I've found the tools to refocus my nurture-balance on a weekly basis.

The Nurturing Continuum

The flow of giving and receiving is essential to our wellbeing. As women, we represent the cosmic female energy of nurturers. In Kabbalistic terminology, we are receivers. This interplay of giving and receiving is a balancing act that is crucial to our success and happiness. We take care of our needs in order to give to to others; we give to others and receive more in return.

This sounds like a simple enough equation, but it tends to get kind of complicated. What about those people who are endless, bottomless pits of need—the people we take care of who leave us feeling depleted, yet, somehow, simultaneously guilty of not giving enough?

When we give from a whole and healthy part of ourselves, we

give in a way that is well-received and, in turn, is replenishing. When we give out of a sense of guilt, we become depleted by our giving.

This is an equation that works both ways. The best intentions on the part of the giver cannot make up for a lack of desire or ability of the recipient to receive.

In our quest for a perfect nurture-balance, we need to evaluate our relationships and determine whether our giving is enabling us to feel replenished—indicating a healthy relationship—or whether our giving leaves us feeling depleted, suggesting the need for us to create distance so that we can continue to give to others with an open and loving heart.

Again, my challah helped me understand this on a deep and personal level. My recipe on page 173 in this book (best. challah. ever.) is a really big recipe. It makes enough for four challahs— or so I had always thought. For years I would make this challah recipe every week and give away two challahs, keeping only the two I needed for myself and my husband. It gave me so much pleasure to give these challahs away and I never got any complaints from the recipients, either! It was so much fun to think of whom I would gift with fresh homemade challah each week and it made my challah baking practice so much more meaningful, as well.

Well, my family grew and suddenly I needed all those loaves of challah for my own Shabbat table. I really didn't want to stop giving my weekly challah gift so I started making two batches of challah each week. With everything that was going on in my life, this just took me over the edge. My challah making became hurried and stressful and didn't feel nearly as satisfying as it used to. Well, you can guess what happened: I stopped giving away challah—it was just too much for me. Until one Friday, when I got a phone call that a good friend was in the hospital.

Wouldn't it be perfect, I thought, if I could drop off some homemade challah for her family—some tasty love and comfort during a hard time? But my dough had already been made and there was no time to make another batch. I divided my dough into six parts that week and, lo and behold, each of those six challahs were perfect! I was floored. I had thought my challah recipe only made four loaves when it actually made six. Or so I thought.

Years passed, during which I made six challahs each week. Soon, though, I needed all those for my own growing family and, once again, I stopped giving challah away. I'm sure you can guess what happened next. One fine week, my magical challah dough stretched to make eight challahs and I began to give the challah out again. So now, when I give you my recipe, I will tell you that it makes eight perfectly sized loaves. You may just be able to take it further . . . I know I have.

Sometimes, we may think that we don't have enough to give. We extend ourselves past our own resources, feeling depleted by the effort. But, when we dig deeply, we find that we do, in fact, possess the perfect amount to give, right there in our very own dented bowl of love.

Elevated Bread

Challah, as we know it, is essentially bread. Perhaps prettier, sweeter, but really just bread. Yet, it is never called bread. It is called challah. It is special, different than our daily bread.

The Hebrew word for bread is *lechem*. In their Hebrew spelling, challah and lechem are made up of the same first two letters—*Lamed* and *Chet*—; the final letter of each word is their only difference. Lechem ends with a *Final Mem*, whose shape is a closed square, while the word challah ends with the letter *Hei*, which is open on its left side and bottom.

The story of the world's creation is one of speech: *"G-d spoke and it came into being" (Tehillim 33:9)*. Each letter of the Hebrew alphabet, therefore, presents us with worlds of meaning.

In the story of letters and words being the tools of creation, the four letters of the Tetragrammaton, the name of G-d that represents His infinite potential and light, play an all-important role. They are the letters through which Divine energy constantly flows into this world, creating it anew at each moment. One of these four letters, the letter *Hei*, is the letter of both giving and receiving. The *Hei* has a perfect flow. It receives from above and then, in turn, gives to below. And this cycle is continuous and perfect.

This *Hei* in the flow of creation is the same *Hei* as in the word challah, transforming it from ordinary lechem into extraordinary challah. Challah may look like bread but it is really so much more than that. Challah is baked in large batches, always served in pairs, and is never just about our own personal survival. The very word challah, which comes from the Torah in the directive to separate the first of our dough as a gift, indicates that this loaf is selected and sacred. When we take off a small piece of the dough and declare it to be the separated challah gift, we are testifying to the fact that we are aware of a larger reality, something bigger than ourselves and our own physical needs.

Transcendence in Our Tents

When our Holy Temple stood, challah was gifted to the priests who served without thought of their own sustenance and therefore required the gifts of others. The Torah, however, speaks of the challah being a gift for the future, as well, preparing us for a time when there would be no Temple, no priest, and, yet, the challah would be as relevant as ever.

During Temple times, spirituality seemed to be something lived outside of one's self. The Temple was an address for holiness, the priest was the person who represented the Divine here on Earth and, in order to achieve connection, a person would travel outside of his or her home to another place.

With the destruction of the Holy Temple and this way of life, our awareness of spirituality and how we were to achieve connection needed to experience a shift. When we no longer had a Temple to travel to nor a priest to turn to, we became compelled to turn inward and find that we ourselves are priests, our own homes holy temples, and that the greatest connectivity possible is always right here, within our hearts and minds.

Infinite Awareness

This awareness that our physical space and actions are the ultimate breeding ground for deep spiritual connection is a reality that was first recognized by women, as is evidenced throughout our storied history.

We learn of our foremother Sarah's tent as a place of life-sustaining miracles: the Cloud of Glory that rested above it, the candles that remained constantly lit within it, and the bread she baked, which never grew stale.

These miracles are indicative of Sarah's life experience. She lived with a constant awareness of the world of spirit while cultivating her physical surroundings: In her relationship with her husband, there was a "Cloud of Glory" that rested above, indicating the presence of the Shechinah, the feminine aspect of Divine that rests in a place of perfect harmony. In her surroundings, the small confines of her open tent, she created a place of beauty, the ever-burning candles representative of a physical grace that transcends its earthly reality and becomes something endlessly alive. In her nurturing of her family, the bread she baked to feed them was infused with a love and care for their spiritual wellbeing as well as their physical bodies. As such, this bread became transcendent of its earthly properties and did not "die" as physical things do, yet stayed fresh and alive from baking to baking.

Such is our power as women: to nurture others in a way that is much more than just the physical feeding and caring of them. Through our awareness of a transcendent reality, we connect the ones we love to the Source of life and love that is beyond the material world and raise them to recognize themselves as more than physical bodies, mere collections of matter, but as G-dly, elevated beings—including, as ever, ourselves in this transformation. The practice of baking challah and the separation of the "challah gift" are our gateways into this awareness.

"Boi Kallah Shabbat Malkata"
ENTER, OH BRIDE, THE SHABBAT QUEEN

— Rabbi Shlomo HaLevi Alkabetz
(C. 5260-5340)

Chapter II
Shabbat, Challah & Woman
: Three of a kind

RISING

Shabbat observed in its fullness is something, much like sleeping and eating, that we have to get to adulthood to fully appreciate.

When my children were little, I made sure to hoard all special treats for Shabbat, creating an excuse for them to crave the sweetness of the day. It has been a tremendous source of *nachat* for me to watch my children grow to delight in the inherent sanctity of the day of Shabbat, although the addition of a great dessert never hurts, either!

As I light the candles on Friday evening, the sky outside is painted in a wash of soft pinks and lavenders and an incredible feeling of relief rushes over me. There is nothing left to be done. All of creation is perfect right now. And, for the next 25 hours, I do not have to think about doing anything, creating, or deconstructing. All is perfect as is. I can just *be* and reconnect with myself and my Maker.

All week, we are busy doing and creating but, while doing so, we are not entirely connected to who we are at our essence. Our workweek reality labels us in terms of what we do: "I'm a doctor, teacher, etc.," or, in terms of our relationships, "I'm her mother, his daughter, her sister . . . ." All of these terms describe us in relation to things that are outside of us and we sometimes lose ourselves in these descriptions. We think we really are a doctor or a wife and this becomes our definition. We reject the wholeness of our inner selves and forget that, aside from all descriptions, we are the essential soul we were born with and will own for the rest of our lives.

On Shabbat, we return to our essential selves. The fact that we cannot create anything new on Shabbat means that we, and the world, have the permission to simply exist, exactly as we are, for this one day of the week.

What a relief!

When we take six strands of dough that we created with our own hands and braid them together, we are bringing together the six days of the week—of working and striving and creating—and gathering them into one perfect whole, the day of Shabbat.

The many restrictions of Shabbat that, to a child or newcomer to the tradition, seem to be a series of "nos," actually create an oasis. It's never about the "no"; it's about the space that is created when all that other stuff is removed.

In college, while studying communication design, the Drawing 101 instructor began the very first class by telling us that we were going to learn a new way of seeing. We were given pencils and papers and instructions to sit in a circle around the center of the room, which contained nothing but a chair. The instructor told us not to look at the chair itself; we could only draw the "negative space" around the chair. Lo and behold, while focusing on the negative space, the perfect shape of a chair emerged. Turns out, it had never been about the negative space; it had been about how to find the shape that was formed within it. Such is the day of Shabbat: a series of restrictions and fences, creating a perfect oasis in time.

Shabbat and Challah

During their forty years of desert wanderings, the Jewish people were deeply aware of the Source of their sustenance. Each morning, they awoke and found a fresh layer of *manna*, heaven-sent bread, a perfect nutrient source, protected by dew and ready to nourish and sustain them. Each day, exactly enough manna for that day would fall, compelling a tremendous trust in the continuous flow of their life-sustaining food. Only on Friday was an extra measure of manna given and collected, eliminating the need to gather on Shabbat. As such, manna became the symbol of our connection and gratitude to the ultimate Source of all our sustenance.

The two challahs on our Shabbat table symbolize the double portion of manna, the original Shabbat bread, and are powerful reminders of the bond of trust and gratitude that lies at the very essence of this day. When we separate this day of the week – Shabbat – and use it to reconnect with the Source of all the gifts we received during the week, we remember that we, too, stem from this Source.

The sanctification of one day of the week is much like the removal of the piece of challah. We declare that this day, and this piece of dough, is separated and holy. And it reminds us that all the other dough, and all days of the week, are sourced in holiness, as well.

Just as the separated ounce of challah reminds us of the higher origin of all our bread and nourishment, Shabbat is a deep declaration of trust and gratitude in our Source of sustenance as something beyond us and bigger than us. While we need to put ourselves out there and make a vessel for sustenance to come in, we always need to remember that, ultimately, our livelihood is not in our control. The sustenance we receive is a Divine gift. And our abstention from work on Shabbat is the ultimate statement of reliance upon and thankfulness for it.

Shabbat and Woman

Shabbat is always referred to in the feminine sense: *Shabbat Hamalka*/ Shabbat the queen. Its energy is visually represented by the image of a queen, and the energy of the day of Shabbat is that of *malchut*/royalty or receptivity. It is the vessel that receives all energy from the previous week and is impregnated with the possibilities of the week to come. Shabbat and challah and the woman all embody the qualities of receiving and gratitude.

We are taking off a piece of our basic nutrient staple, the dough for the bread with which we intend to feed our family, implying an awareness that the source of this sustenance transcends our efforts. As such, the separation of challah represents implicit trust and gratitude, gratitude being the capacity to acknowledge the source of our gifts and express thankfulness for them. These are both inherently feminine characteristics as outlined in Kabbalistic teachings.

An important note to my readers: Throughout this book, when speaking of masculine and feminine energies as outlined and depicted in Kabbalistic teachings, I am not speaking exclusively of either a man or a woman. The Torah acknowledges that man and woman each contain both energies within them: *"[Z]achar u-nekeiva bara otam/[M]ale and female He created them"* (Bereishit 1:27).

Masculine and feminine energies working in tandem enliven each of us, to a lesser or greater degree. However, "woman" becomes a prototype of female energy, and this is reflected in her biological makeup, as well. The same for "man" with male energy and male biology.

Woman and Challah

Our first pronouncement upon awakening each day is one of gratitude to our Creator for giving us a new day, expressed in the short prayer beginning with the words *"Modeh ani lefanecha/*I am grateful before You."* These three words of gratitude have a combined numerical value of 306, equal to the numerical value of the word *isha/*woman.

In the Hebrew alphabet, some letters are energetically masculine and some are feminine. The letter *Hei* [ה], which transforms daily lechem into challah, is a feminine letter that represents gratitude and receptivity. It is also the letter that changes the word *ish* [איש]/man to *isha*[אשה]/woman.

Hei is the letter of creation and creativity, a function that both receives and gives forth. It is an ability to receive in a way that is also giving, much as the woman who receives the initial seed of life is able to actualize it and bring forth a living being.

"The man brings the wheat home, but does he chew wheat? He brings in the flax, but can he wear flax?" (Talmud, Yevamot 63a).

The woman is the one who takes the raw materials of life and makes them nourishing, comforting, and life-sustaining. The female aspect of receptivity is not a passive pose; it is proactive and productive.

The idea of receiving as the deepest form of giving is something that we have hopefully each experienced at some point in our lives. On a very practical level, there are those who are able to receive what we give them—be it an expression of our emotions towards them or a physical gift—in a manner that makes us feel like we are the ones who have been given something.

Letting Go a Little

The letter *Hei* is fascinating in that it is both silent and vocal. It is used at the end of a word as a silent, supporting letter, and in the beginning or center of a word as a vocal, expressive letter.

The *Hei's* dual functions serve as a great lesson in creativity and receptivity.

To truly create, we need to be present—the fullness of our whole self must come forth—but we must also step aside to allow for the creation to occur. The combination of full expression coupled with complete humility allows for a new entity to emerge.

As a professional artist, I have often puzzled over the elusive creative process, which I must access each day to do my job as a designer, artist, and writer. It occurred to me quite early in my career as a graphic artist that the more my ego was attached to the project at hand, the more difficulty I would have accessing my creativity. If I was worrying about how the client was going to like the finished piece, or whether it would appear that I was an accomplished artist (yay!) or a fraudulent wannabe (oops!), I would get stuck and be unable to create something "fresh." It was only after letting go of my attachment to the outcome and allowing the ideas to flow through me that I could truly be creative. Of course, this flow was occurring after years of training and on-the-job experience, all of which were very much a part of me, but, at the moment of creation, there was no expression of that, just a removal of ego from the story.

I have often seen this and I'm sure you must have have, also: a couple tries so hard to conceive a child, to no avail, only to suddenly find themselves pregnant after taking a break from "trying" or once they've decided to adopt. What has happened? Quite simply, they have removed their attachment to the outcome from the process and made room for creation to occur.

Our forefather Avraham and foremother Sarah were childless and unable to conceive until G-d gifted them each with the letter *Hei*. Avram became *Avraham*, with the expressive and vocal *Hei*, while Sarai became *Sarah*, with the silent *Hei*. It was then that the creation of a child was possible.

The woman, the challah, and Shabbat are all expressions of the silent *Hei* of creation, the quality of gratitude and receptivity. The receiving is so powerful and fully absorbed that it brings forth new creation.

"The good life is a process, not a state of being. It is a direction, not a destination."
— Carl Rogers

"THE ART OF COOKERY IS THE CONSTANT EXPRESSION OF THE PRESENT."
— AUGUSTE ESCOFFIER, FRENCH CHEF

Chapter III
Living in the Process
and Loving every Moment

"The reward of a mitzvah is the mitzvah itself."
— Avot 4:2

RISING

We live in a fast-moving world.

It's a world of information downloaded at the speed of light, of travel from one end of the planet to the other in the space of day, and of technology that progresses so quickly, it's making the twenty-somethings seem old. Everything needs to happen immediately, if not sooner. Patience and longing seem to be emotional relics of the past. And, truthfully, as a person living fully in this generation, I think you'll agree with me that there's nothing quite as frustrating as that little color wheel (hourglass, loading line . . .) that shows up on our screens and tells us that we have to . . . wait?!

We buy new appliances, new gadgets with the promises of faster, more immediate results. If that doesn't happen immediately, we move onto the next web page, the faster lane, the drive-thru . . . . These are symptoms of a result-oriented and, *dare I say it*, male-oriented society.

This world was created in a manner that calls for our involvement in its perpetuation. Our input drives the evolution of physics, technology, medicine, and the arts, and yet, woven into the very fabric of creation, is Shabbat, a Divinely ordained day of rest.

Weekday reality is one of productivity and proactive creativity. During the six days of the week, we are called upon to use our unique gifts to effect change in our surroundings. When Shabbat arrives, we are summoned to accept all that exists at that very moment as perfection. We are not meant to change anything.

Shabbat reality is one of stillness and deep appreciation of the inherent unity of all that exists, as it is, right now.

Kabbalah/the Jewish mystical tradition explains that the Creator creates and sustains the world through a delicate balance of male and female energies, with the male element being that of a giver and the female, the receiver. The world is infused with a "giving" male quality and sustained by a "receiving" female quality.

The workweek is the expression of the male, "giving" energy in the universe, while Shabbat is where the female expression of receiving is welcomed and sustained. It is precisely this interplay of the workweek and Shabbat, the balance between ambition and satisfaction, creativity and receptivity, exhale and inhale, that keeps the world in a healthy equilibrium.

We live in world that still largely believes itself to be in survival mode, a "dog eat dog" reality as it were, where ego is king and productivity is measured in numbers. In this society, we have come to value the male, result-oriented weekday energy as making more of a significant contribution to the development of our world than the female, sustaining Shabbat energy, though, in truth, both are equally vital.

Honoring the Process

In the role of nurturer, so much of what is accomplished is immediately undone. We wash a dish, only to have it dirtied once again. We make a bed only to have it slept in again, do the laundry only to have it be worn again, and listen empathetically to our child or friend only to have him or her cry about something else (or, more likely, the very same thing!) the next day.

RISING

When our day-jobs consist of clients and tasks to be completed and the items we tick off on our to-do lists actually stay done, we may find ourselves lured to the male, result-oriented reality, and understandably so. However, allowing ourselves to be tied closely to results in all areas of life will leave us continuously disappointed and wanting during our "off-work" hours.

What if we could enter, for at least part of the day, into the feminine, sustaining reality and fully be in that place? What if the point of washing the dish is the washing itself, not the clean dish that results? What if the point of listening is just the listening—being fully present for the person in front of us—not the offering of solutions?

The practice of separating the challah is unique amongst other Jewish rituals in that it is one that occurs mid-process. We don't wait for the fully braided, egged, and baked challahs to emerge from the oven before reciting the blessing. Rather, we honor the process of the baking by removing a piece of the unbaked and unformed dough and reciting a blessing specifically at that time.

Challah baking is unique in that, regardless of modern technology and time-saving techniques, it is still a process that requires our presence and participation. When we put our hands into the challah bowl and knead the ingredients together, we actively participate in the feeding of our families. And, when we direct our focus and intention into the combining of the ingredients, we raise our own awareness of this nurturing and provide our families with more of ourselves.

In my challah classes I often encounter comments such as, "You are a professional. My challahs are not going to look like that," or, "Look at my challah, it looks your challah's uglier little sister," or, "I have a PhD in English Literature but I have no degree in baking. This is just not going to work."

My response to these comments has been, and continues to be, that the deepest connection, the mitzvah of separating challah, occurs long before the challah looks pretty or otherwise. This suggests that the gift of the challah occurs within the process of making the challah. Nobody's dough is inherently prettier than the next person's. It's not about the finished product. When we are fully present during the process, the results—though they may not be "perfect looking"—will be a flawless reflection of our love and care. And, therefore, the challah is perfect.

This idea holds true, so true, in the raising of our children and the nurturing of our loved ones. When we parent and nurture with our whole being and focus on the process rather than try to achieve desired results, we find that the results end up being sweet and perfect.

The Power of Presence

How often, in our rush to get to the next thing, do we hurry along our loved ones, sometimes saying the words "hurry up" more frequently than we say "I love you"? We often forget that the magic is happening in the moment, right before our very eyes. We just need to stop and be there—to bring all of ourselves to that very instant and be totally and completely present.

A funny thing happened at the Western Wall.

It was the spring of 2009 and my first time back in Jerusalem since I had stood at the Wall as a pimply teenager, praying for things I couldn't even fathom.

This time, my prayers and my life had changed beyond recognition. I was old enough to understand what I was praying for and clear-skinned enough to know that everything heals with time. It was at that moment that I heard my name being called from somewhere behind me. I turned around and saw a woman I had met many years earlier. She had lived near us in Brooklyn at least ten years prior and had eventually emigrated to Jerusalem, as many of our congregants have done over the years. I remembered her as a "wild child," a party-loving college grad who was always seeking the next thrill. She looked different now, centered and serene.

After dispensing with the hugs and exclamations, I asked her what she was up to and why she looked so changed.

Her next words truly surprised me. "Remember when, eight years ago, I came to speak privately with you and shared the difficulties I was going through at the time?" I did remember. Quite clearly in fact, as it was early in my days of growing a community and I remember the overwhelming feeling of responsibility (and intimidation) I felt when someone asked for my(!) advice. "That meeting with you changed the entire direction of my life," she continued. "I moved to Israel, started studying, and my whole center of being shifted."

I will admit to having experienced a moment of pride right then, as I imagined that I had told her something so earth-shattering that it had changed the course of her entire life. Well, my pride was properly put into place because when I asked her what it was that I had told her, she answered, "I actually don't remember a word you said."

Hmm. So much for my theory of myself as wise sage. She continued to say, with tears in her eyes, that, "it wasn't the words you said [those "brilliant" words that I stayed up all night formulating, mind you], it was just the fact that at the moment of our meeting, I truly felt that there was nobody else on Earth besides for you and me. I felt important and recognized and this turned out to be the turning point in my spiritual journey."

Such is the power of being present. Just you and I, wholly and completely in the moment. Nothing else matters.

According to the sages of the Talmud *(Nedarim 20b)*, the ideal moment for conception occurs when man and woman are fully and completely focused on each other. With no thoughts of any other person, and nothing in the world existing but the two of them, they create and draw down a new soul and life that is perfect and whole.

When our loved ones see that the buzzing phone distracts us from them, it reduces their feeling of mattering. When our children observe that our attention is always divided, they absorb the message that they are not so important. When the one we love walks through the door and we put down the phone so that we can be there for him or her, we are making a powerful statement that reverberates for life, louder than the ringing, buzzing, or beeping of any electronic device.

We don't need to graduate Le Cordon Bleu to bake a challah, much as we generally don't earn a PhD in child psychology before we parent. We go through this life armed with ourselves . . . and that's it. But, when we truly connect with our inner selves and respect the gift that bringing this whole self to the table truly is, we create something beautiful. The challahs that are baked with care, much like the child raised with the blessing of his or her parents' full presence of being, are perfect creations and they will rise.

A Life Lived Fully

I want to tell you about my mother-in-law, of blessed memory. I called her *Shvigger*, a guttural-sounding Yiddish word for mother-in-law that became beautiful to me by association. My shvigger was my greatest role model for a person who gives the most singular gift in life by her very presence. Her parenting model was far from conventional, yet she raised incredibly confident, self-respecting, and happy children. She did so simply by being completely and ecstatically herself and being fully present for her loved ones.

Her home was her castle, her kingdom the kitchen table, and, sitting there, over countless mugs of coffee and chocolate jelly rings, I learned the invaluable lessons of a life lived fully.

The work of the priests in the Temple is often compared to the traditional work of the nurturer—that of caring for, comforting, and feeding one's family. The work of the priests was mostly menial and repetitive. They were, quite literally, getting their hands dirty in the service of G-d. And with each sweep of their brooms, with each cleaning of the altar, they declared that this work was Divine service, and it truly was. In fact, it was this menial work that hinged the connection of the entire Jewish nation with G-d. As nurturers, serving in our own mini temples, when we are continuously aware that the work of our hands and of our hearts is a form of Divine expression and connection, we are living fully.

When the Torah lists long life as a reward for the fulfillment of specific mitzvot, the term used is *"length of days" (Devarim 11:21)*. Indeed, those words contain the key to a fulfilled and wholesome life: a life in which each day is filled to capacity. While we pray to attain long years, we can only choose to act upon that which is within our power and acquire long days.

A long (i.e. full) day is one in which we are completely present at every given moment. It is a day during which I waste no time worrying about that mother in PTA who may (or may not) have been judging me for my choice of outfit, a day during which I don't simply hope for time to pass so I can get to the next stop on my itinerary, a day during which I simply live each moment. If it is a PTA meeting, I am fully there for my child. If I am in traffic, I can allow myself to be in my thoughts and focus on whatever it is I'd like to think about instead of simply waiting for the next car to move, the next light to change, and the traffic to clear.

Perhaps this is why time moves faster for adults than for children. Small children don't waste time thinking of end results or others' judgments; they are too busy living fully in each moment and, as such, each moment is complete. Each breath is filled with wonder, each tick of the clock an opportunity, every step an excuse for discovery, every day a lifetime.

My shvigger, to our deep sorrow, did not live a conventionally long life, but it was a life lived so fully and completely—no time wasted on regret—that she may have well lived a hundred and twenty years.

As we knead the challah dough, we put our arms, hearts, and minds into the process. Not waiting for it to be "over with" so we can eat the challah, we are mindful of the process of creating the dough itself.

We take a piece of the raw dough and recite a blessing. As in all aspects of our lives, it is the raw material from which we create and shape and form, and it is upon this unfinished and unformed dough that we recite a blessing. As we separate the dough, we draw blessing down into our sustenance, homes, and lives, grateful for the process of living, and praying for a life lived fully.

"THE MEETING OF TWO PERSONALITIES IS LIKE THE CONTACT OF TWO CHEMICAL SUBSTANCES, IF THERE IS ANY REACTION, BOTH ARE TRANSFORMED."

—JUNG

Chapter IV
Setting the Stage
: an Environment for Rising

*"...Man does not live by bread alone, but rather by what emanates
from the mouth of Hashem does man live."*

— Devarim, 8:3

RISING

At the court of Rabbi Schneur Zalman of Liadi, the great Chasidic master also known as the Alter Rebbe (lit. old master), there was a chasid, Reb Shmuel Munkes, who was a great and learned man in his own right. He had the temperament of a jolly jester and, as such, was often employed to help lighten the atmosphere. Indeed, many an opportunity lent itself to his wittiness and humor.

At one particular farbrengen (Chasidic gathering), Reb Shmuel Munkes was asked to recite some words of wisdom. The assembled crowd waited in anticipation to hear something lighthearted and witty. To their surprise, this time Reb Shmuel began describing a process that sounded quite esoteric and confusing to them.

Reb Shmuel began: "There was a scattering of particles that merged with the source of life, pure water, to create a great circle of being. This great circle of being was then drawn down into individual strands of energy, allowing themselves to be formed and finally to be drawn through a refinement of fire, wherein the particles were finally fit to be absorbed."

A great silence filled the room. "That's it?!" The chasidim, having hoped for some lighthearted wisdom, turned in confusion to the Rebbe, who, with a twinkle in his eye, revealed the punchline. "Reb Shmuel," the Rebbe said with a smile, "has just given us his wife's challah recipe."

As the great Chasidic masters understood, the cosmic story of the creation of all life is, in fact, just like making a batch of challah.

The recipe for bread is quite simple. The most basic bread recipe requires only two primary ingredients: flour and water. And these two simple ingredients come together to create something much grander than the sum of their parts. There is nothing extra or unnecessary here. Each ingredient is a crucial part of the whole and each one relies on the other to create a living, breathing dough that will rise.

As challah baking became part of my weekly routine, it seemed to merge with all other aspects of my life. Birth, babies, marriage and work-life balance, all of life's hard earned lessons, it seemed, could be gleaned from this ball of dough rising before me. My very prayers, in fact, were influenced and enhanced by this weekly practice of creating challah. Now, on Friday eve, as the sun begins to set and I create a private space between my hands and my eyes, I light the Shabbat candles and pray that my children will rise.

It is a deceptively simple prayer, one that holds within it a world of meaning. My most heartfelt prayer is that my children be deeply rooted in an environment of trust and sweetness, and that this become their foundation of confidence so they can then be passionate about their lives and their connection to G-d, live comfortably and joyously with their spiritual and material realities hand in hand, and strive to constantly expand and rise.

This is my prayer. These are my psalms. *Please, G-d, let them rise.*

There is so much that we can't control in this life. The further along in life we are, the more power we cede to a Higher Source. Yet, with all that we can't control, there is an area in which we have been granted immense power, namely, in our role as nurturers. We have been given an almost G-dly faculty to infuse others with a joy for life and a confidence in the knowledge that they are perfect and whole and capable of rising.

The recipe for challah appeared to me as the perfect role model toward creating an environment for rising as I strove to create such a context for myself and my family. Somewhere in this simple recipe for bread, that would rise and become a challah, I would find the recipe for rising in life. I would elevate my existence beyond the everyday, shaping a life lived to its fullest.

As we merge the ingredients to create our challah, we meditate on each addition, opening ourselves to fresh outlook and insight into our nourishing and nurturing.

I will share with you the insights that came to me over years of challah baking and child raising; incredibly, somewhere between diaper changes and homework, these can actually happen! I suspect, however, that as you begin your own tradition of challah, you will find yourself with plenty of your own epiphanies and "aha" moments. Relish these moments of inspiration in a full and busy life; it is a blessing to stumble upon these sparks of insight, and a particular blessing when these occur in your very own kitchen, somewhere deep within your challah bowl.

"If there is no flour,

there is no Torah."

—Avot 3:17

Flour
: scattered particles

To create a challah, we begin with flour, the most substantial in-gredient of physical sustenance. After all, bread is the staff of life.

The sages of the Mishnah write, "*[I]m ein kemach, ein Torah/* [W]ithout flour, there is no Torah" *(Avot 3:17)*. The physical needs of the body must be taken care of in order to realize its higher functions.

Flour represents the physical body of a person, as well as the body of humanity as a whole. In this tangible, material world we experience reality as separation, much like the individuated particles of flour. We feel ourselves to be separate from others, we experience physical objects as unrelated to each other; each thing seems to exist separately and individually. Our five senses inform us that this thing is red and that thing is blue. This thing smells great and this other thing, not so much. It is this essential brokenness that we strive to heal throughout our lives, reconcil-ing the scattered particles of ourselves and our perceptions into a greater unity.

RISING

When we think of our own health and survival, it is very much about ourselves against the world. It is about "I need to survive, at any cost."

In the spiritual nurturing of ourselves and our loved ones, while we focus on our well-being, health, and material satisfaction, we know deeply all the while that, in a fully realized life, this is but one piece of a much larger picture.

Flour without water will forever remain a mere collection of individual particles—dry, separate and unable to rise. They will remain unelevated sparks, waiting to merge with the great Oneness, the Source of all life.

Though our Sages say, *"[I]m ein kemach ein Torah/*[W]ithout flour there is no Torah," they continue by saying, *"im ein Torah, ein kemach/*without Torah, there is no flour." Herein lies a symbiotic relationship; one does not exist without the other.

Interestingly, *chitah*, the Hebrew word for wheat, the origin of flour, has the numeric value of 22. The number 22 represents the 22 letters of the Hebrew alphabet, which combine to create the Torah and are through which the world was created and is sustained. This demonstrates that *kemach*/flour, which is made of wheat, is an essential building block in creation.

When there is no flour, there is no Torah. When we are in survival mode, struggling to simply exist, and do not have the kemach to sustain our bodies, there is no room in our minds for meaning and higher purpose. In order to live a life of expanded awareness, we must take care to nurture the body and cultivate our material existence. The body and the soul, the flour and water, must coexist, each supporting the needs of the other.

The concept of separateness returning to a state of wholeness is a recurring theme throughout Judaism and particularly so in the deeper mystical wisdom. We find many traditions of acknowledging the brokenness—even, and particularly—during our most ecstatic moments of joy. In seeking to create wholeness, we must first be aware of the separations and, from that place, strive to create completion.

At the height of our most joyful moment, the culmination of the *chuppah* and the joining of two souls to create a perfect union, we shatter a glass, acknowledging that this union will be another attempt to bring healing to the fragmentation that is inherent in the physical aspects of life. We wish the couple *mazal tov* immediately afterward, wishing them good *mazal*/luck, in achieving this lofty goal together.

Adam and Eve existed in an idyllic state, a paradise in which all was clearly connected to the Tree of Life, a reality of perfect unity. When they ate from the forbidden tree, the Tree of Knowledge (of good and evil) they were exposed to and internalized the reality of separation and duality, a world in which there is good and evil, life and death.

There are sages who interpret the fruit of the Tree of Knowledge as the wheat stalk. While many sages differ as to the exact nature of the fruit of the Tree of Knowledge, all agree that the shattering of the Garden of Eden's perfect unity when the forbidden fruit was eaten, took place mere moments before the first Shabbat began.

In this interpretation, wheat, the basis of our challah dough, is the very "fruit" that brought about the original separation, changing the state of the world from a "Tree of Life" state of perfect unity to a "Tree of Knowledge" world of separation. As such, the baking of challah, done as a preparation for Shabbat, becomes the *tikkun*, the healing, for the original brokenness and separation. an undoing of the eating from the Tree of Knowledge and a re-entering into the Tree of Life.

"My teaching
shall drip
like rain;
My word will
flow like dew;
...and like
raindrops
on grass

—Devarim 32:2

Water
:the great merging

"Ein mayim ela Torah/Water refers to Torah"
— *Bava Kamma 17a*

How do we cohere all that separateness?

With water.

"The world was void and nothingness... and the spirit of Elokim hovers on the face of the water" (Bereishit 1:2).

It is the first mention of water in the Torah, yet no reference to its creation precedes this pronouncement. The first creation that is spoken into being, "Let there be light," occurs after the presence—and, therefore, creation—of water has already been established.

Water is primordial; it is the fount of all creation and continuously gives life to all of existence. All life begins with water and all life is supported by water. We enter the waters of the *mikvah* (ritual bath) before creating new life; new life emerges from the waters of the womb. We greet each new day of our lives with purifying waters and, on our very last day, we are immersed into water one final time before being laid to rest.

We can understand why water is compared to Torah and the life of the soul. In its continuous flow and unbrokenness since the beginning of time, water gives us a glimpse into immortality. It is a place of endless hope and eternal life. All water that exists today has existed since the beginning of time and will continue its life cycle of evaporation, condensation and life-giving precipitation.

When the Torah speaks of purity and impurity, it is simply speaking of that which is connected to life and that which is not. Life, or purity, represents all that is growing, hopeful, and eternal. The opposite of life, which is impurity, represents a state of separation, stagnation, and despair.

In Jewish practice, water is continually used for purification, i.e., to bring something from a state of separation back into a state of unified oneness. Water represents an ultimate life force that has the capacity of unifying the scattered and broken.

In all the great transitions of life, historically and in our everyday existence, we have used, and continue to use, water to connect endings and beginnings, beginnings and endings. Water eases the transition and creates a merging of the two ends, bringing wholeness.

In the days of Noah and the Great Flood, a melding of higher and lower waters brought a purification to the world, changing the face of the earth and bringing healing. The Hebrews crossed the waters of the Red Sea to leave slavery and enter a state of freedom. The waters of the Jordan needed to be crossed before coming into our nationhood in our own land. In all the transitions of our lives, from night to day, loss to life, weekday to Shabbat, *mayim chayim*, the living waters of the mikvah—either gathered into a man-made pool, or expressed in nature as oceans or lakes—can bring us from a state of separation back into our original state of wholeness.

When Flour and Water Combine

Flour is the body, the material, which without water is simply scattered particles, not nourishing, and wholly indigestible. Water is the soul, the spiritual, which without flour cannot express itself and is not able to nourish properly. The flour mixed with the water creates something that is alive and can feed us. The body, which contains a soul, has the capacity to express itself and live. Each needs the other to create a perfect circle of wholeness.

When we combine water and flour, we unite all the scattered pieces of existence and create something whole and alive.

Remember those strands mentioned by Reb Shmuel Munkes in his challah recipe of creation—the strands of living energy created from the water merging with the scattered particles? When flour and water merge, something magical begins to happen: gluten swells to form a continuous network of fine strands and the flour and water begin to rise. The physical and spiritual reality, living hand in hand, side by side, merge to become the embodiment of the *Igul haGadol*/the Great Circle of Being that contains within it the potential of all life and reality.

All it takes is flour, water, and time, and rising happens.

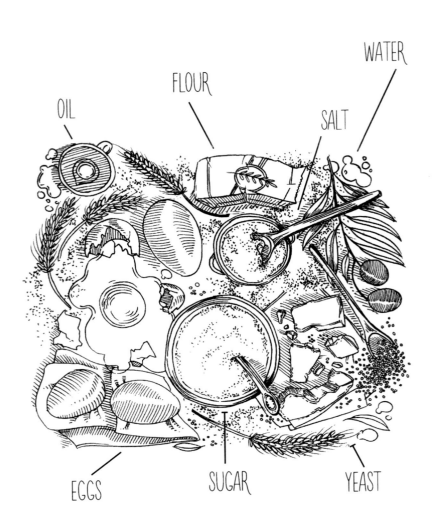

OIL

FLOUR

WATER

SALT

EGGS

SUGAR

YEAST

Chapter V
The Ingredients
:a Recipe for Rising

RISING

The very first woman, Chava (Eve), is called "em kol chai/the mother of all living things," before she ever gives birth.

Each woman is born with all the eggs she will have throughout her life. That is to say that all our mothering potential is input into our very beings before we ever mother and regardless of whether we indeed end up "mothering" in the traditional sense of the word. As women, we are the nurturers of creation, we bring forth life in countless ways, and the ways we nurture are as vast and varied as the ways through which we bring forth life.

There are the basics that we are given at birth: a body and a soul, our "flour and water" as it were. And then, there are the gifts we acquire along the way that create a life that is uniquely ours and unmistakably individual. These are the gifts we bring to the table when we nurture others. And while the recipe for nurturing, much like a challah recipe, always looks the same when spelled out, in practice, each person will nurture with his or her unique qualities. If fully and joyfully expressed, this will be the greatest gift he or she can ever give.

While parenting, we have, for many years, been drowning out our inner voices with the voices of others. We read Dr. Spock and put our babies to sleep on their stomachs, only to quickly flip them onto their backs when the newest studies indicated that this is the safest way. With the advent of the Google "gods," we are more inundated than ever with "expert" parenting advice. At last count, Amazon's parenting and relationship sections boasted 717,073 selections, not including the many millions of web pages devoted to this ever confusing and evolving topic. "Parenting by Google" is now a thing, according to some of my new-parent friends who are actually doing this.

Baby is spitting up a weird color? Quick! Google it! My toddler just said "no" to me? Google it! But, sadly, the plethora of differing opinions, each one claiming to be unequivocally true, often just leads to further confusion.

Listening to our Inner Voice

"*Every day a bat kol goes forth from Mount Sinai . . .*" *(Avot 6:2).* This *bat kol*, or voice, beckons us to our deepest reality.

We are all equipped with an incredible inner receptor to this voice of the *bat kol*. Heeding this voice, we are guided by it; it is a deeper listening to the reverberation of the vibrations of Sinai during the time we received Divine wisdom in our lives. The bat kol is a femininely termed name, literally translated as "*daughter of the voice,*" for it is a gentle echo, a receiving, continuation, and realization of the wisdom of Sinai. The bat kol lives inside each of us and, if we can tune in to its vibrations, we can access its eternal wisdom.

Sounds too incredible?

Consider this: how often do we look to others for answers, only to speak with a really good listener and discover that the answers were within us all along and we simply didn't take the time to listen and acknowledge our own inherent wisdom? Most of the time, we actually know the answers to our deepest questions; they are part of who we are. In reaching deep down to our bat kol we can access them and integrate them into our lives.

When we nurture our families, we are often at a loss for what to do next. As soon as we feel like we are getting the hang of nurturing a spouse, we become partners in raising a new life and need to relearn the art. Just as we begin to feel proficient in the newborn stage, suddenly she's an infant, and then, all too quickly, a toddler, a teenager, an adult. . . . Life moves quickly and we want quick answers.

When we take the time to bake our challah, and place ourselves fully in the process, we find ourselves accessing our very own answers, our own deep intuitive knowledge, which tells us we have the tools we need to get this right and do it with joy and fullness of being. Just lean in and listen closely. Pour in each ingredient and focus on the recipe for nurturing in your very own way, rediscovering and rethinking each part of the recipe each time you go back to your challah bowl. Each new week of baking brings with it new realizations and new opportunities for exploring the way we have been doing things, allowing us to determine whether we need to find new direction.

We've spoken about the flour and water, the basics that we are born with. Now let's talk about the other stuff.

"WITH BREAD **YEAST** & HUMANS, THERE ARE ABOUT 45 AMINO ACIDS THAT ARE DIFFERENT AND ABOUT 59 THAT ARE IDENTICAL. THINK HOW CLOSE TOGETHER MAN AND THIS OTHER ORGANISM,

BREAD YEAST, ARE. WHAT IS THE PROBABILITY THAT IN 59 POSITIONS THE SAME CHOICE OUT OF 20 POSSIBILITIES WOULD HAVE BEEN MADE BY ACCIDENT? IT IS IMPOSSIBLY SMALL . . . AND SO WE SEE THAT NOT ONLY ARE ALL MEN BROTHERS, BUT MEN AND **YEAST** CELLS, TOO. . . ."

— LINUS PAULING, GREAT AMERICAN CHEMIST, 1933

Yeast

While rising will naturally occur when flour and water are left to their own devices, this can be quite a lengthy process. The advent of adding a previously fermented yeast product has shortened the process and added to the tastiness of the bread, as well.

Yeast is a microscopic single-cell organism that is naturally present in the air. When added to flour and water, it feeds on the sugar in the flour's carbohydrates. As the yeast multiplies and grows, it produces alcohol, which add flavor to the dough, and also carbon dioxide, which creates the structure of the bread.

Carol Field, in her book, *The Italian Baker*,[1] writes that when there is a lot of bread being prepared in one place, there is a high concentration of naturally occurring yeast in the air that adds to the bread.

1 Field, Carol. *The Italian Baker.* New York: Harper & Row, 1985. Print.

The moral of the story is, the more challah you bake in your kitchen, the better your challah will be!

With the availability of commercial yeast, and later, the invention of granulated yeast (courtesy of Charles Fleischmann, a German Jewish immigrant, during the Second World War), the process of rising our dough has been considerably expedited.

A Closer Look

Yeast is an interesting organism that has been given much attention in the Torah. Passover is an entire holiday, in fact, that is dedicated to the avoidance of the fermentation process in general and, more specifically, to the consumption of yeast.

Interestingly, the discovery of yeast as a food fermentation product dates back to ancient Egypt, where our own story began. The Egyptians, most likely having left flour and water outside in the heat, realized that the fermentation leads to a better-risen and more flavorful bread, as well as a really great beverage known as beer . . . so now just imagine that the whole story of our exodus occurred with a thoroughly inebriated Egyptian Pharaoh, but that's for another time.

In the Torah, this rising process represents a rising ego, just as the matzah, flat bread traditionally eaten on Passover, symbolizes an absence of ego, a humility as it were. This is why the Exodus from Egypt, the place of constriction, serves as a metaphor for our own personal release from our ego, which is the root of all perceived limitation. We take a week off from all association with yeast and, therefore, ego, and allow ourselves to re-calibrate our internal rising system.

Balancing Ego

Ego is essential to our survival. Without it, we wouldn't get up in the morning, feed ourselves, go to work or bother to look both ways before crossing the street. The Torah prescribes an eight-day abstention from yeast, a deflating of the ego, that may, with time, become opaque and overly bloated due to perceived threats to its survival when, in fact, there are none. For example, there are times when we walk into a room and think that the people in it are talking about us, affecting our ability to focus and function. That is an expression of an inflamed ego, an exaggerated or skewed sense of our place in this world that leads to an unhealthy relationship with others and the world around us.

Unlike humility, a low self-esteem is actually a sign of an inflated ego. The person perceives all of humanity as a threat or, at the very least, to be revolving around his existence.

With a healthy sense of self, we are comfortable with who we are and are happy with our place in society. From that vantage point, we are comfortable and have a healthy, realistic sense of ourselves. We are able to view the rest of the world as a counterbalance to ourselves. We see every person and situation as someone or something to learn from as we strive to grow and perfect ourselves towards our own tikkun, personal soul elevation and articulation.

The Import of Faith

In raising joyous and confident children, our first job is to give them a healthy sense of self. We do this by acknowledging them as part of the Divine, a perfect gift from above.

Faith is the very first thing a child learns upon entering this world and it is the mother who provides it. It is, much like bread, essential to our survival. In responding to our child's immediate needs, we are able to instill within him a healthy sense of trust and faith in humanity, an inherent knowledge that he is deserving of care and love, and an instinct to trust in goodness.

All the information our children will receive during their lives will be filtered through this lens of trust and faith. It is precisely this faith that will allow them to receive knowledge and integrate it in a healthy way.

Our first and foremost responsibility as nurturers is the transmission of a sense of self-worth and esteem in the people we love and an inherent sense of faith in their inner goodness and wholeness. A person who has received in such a way is capable of giving in much the same way, creating a cycle of love that produces whole and happy human beings. As such, I wholeheartedly believe that the healing of this world will be brought about through the perfect love of each mother to her child, each nurturer to those he or she embraces.

When we think of the brokenness of the world, the fighting within families, the wars, the struggle for power and wealth, it is obvious that the pain is caused by children who have grown into adults never having felt that they are essentially good and whole in the crucial beginnings of their lives. Perhaps this may sound presumptuous or perhaps an oversimplification of a fact. However, it is something that, over my years of nurturing, I have come to understand as a deep, deep truth.

When we are taught to believe that we are whole and complete at our essence, we see the whole world as participating in our growth and sustenance and the world looks back at us in the same way. If we haven't received this knowledge of our inherent positive qualities, there is a shattering. Essentially, this is a breaking of our natural trust in the inherent goodness of ourselves and therefore in others, and a distrust of others is born. All our brokenness and pain in life, aside from circumstances beyond our control, such as, G-d forbid, death or illness, can be traced back to this lack of faith in our own wholeness.

When we decide to believe that we are each a G-d given gift and, as such, wonderful even in our imperfections (which, of course, does not negate the need to constantly grow and better ourselves), we shine a light into this world, one that brings healing and peace to those around us. I have seen it happen countless times. A person who feels secure about himself enters the room and the room lights up. Those in his sphere feel better about themselves just by being in his presence and the effects can be far-reaching.

This innate security that radiates outwards is known in Hebrew as *chein*, an inner light that comes along with a person's outside being aligned with his or her inside. It is a wholeness of self, a deep belief that he or she is lovable and worthy of love, which, in turn, makes him or her lovable and pleasant to others.

Children who are young enough to be un-self-conscious radiate this natural chein; it is what draws us to them and makes them so beloved. They are not worried that something is wrong with them. They know we will love them and they believe themselves to be worthy of that love. And so it is true, we do love them and believe wholeheartedly in their inherent right to adoration.

We don't need to have received this perfectly in our infancy to be able to achieve this state of chein, nor do we need to be in a perfect state of chein to pass it on to those we love.

Second Chances

A frantic call at 3pm on Friday: It is Giselle. She has been coming to my challah class about once a year for the past few years. Challah baking does not come naturally to her but she is heroically determined to master it. In a panicky voice half-hiccupping with despair as I pick up the phone, she blurts out, "My challah dough! It's not rising! It's been an hour and still no sign of rising. I used all the ingredients you told me, I did everything right. What happened?"

We calmly went through all the steps. I had her check the package of yeast she had used. Had it expired, or was it fresh and still "alive"? We determined that indeed the yeast was okay but perhaps the water she had used had been too cold and the environment the dough had been placed in, too dry and cool.

I had her place a pan of boiling water on the bottom of her oven and set her stubborn, unrisen dough into this steamy, sauna-like environment. She shut the oven door. Within moments, the dough was rising.

Sometimes, we don't get it right the first time. We gave it all we had, or perhaps we didn't. Maybe we were distracted, not completely present at the moment. Overwhelmed by the peripherals and unaware that this precious time to create the dough was so short, it passed by quickly and we missed the moment. Whatever the case may be, at some point we see the dough we have created and feel that we have failed. The dough is not rising.

Remember the basic ingredients of challah: flour and water. That's it. All of us already possess these basics ingredients, a body and a soul. Bathed in a conducive environment of moisture, warmth, and sweetness, it will eventually rise. When the dough does not seem to be developing as it should, just remember these three simple elements: water, an environment that is eternally alive with spirituality and connectedness; warmth, an embracing, accepting place; and sweetness, pure kindness and patience. Mix together, give it plenty of time and watch your dough rise.

We don't always remember or know to have given these things when our babies were young, when our marriage was new, when the friendship began. We ourselves may not have received the connectedness, the warmth, and the sweetness. But the lesson in our challah bowl is that it is never too late. It is a constant striving to reach this place of deep faith in ourselves that gives rise to the perfect nurturing of others.

When we put the yeast into our dough, we take the time to focus on our own sense of self-worth and faith in our essential wholeness. We then extend that faith into the ones we love and nurture. We understand that each moment, each day, is a new opportunity for us to instill a deep-seated sense of the inborn wholeness of each person whom we love. With this "bread of faith" we will heal and transform, allowing ourselves and our loved ones and, in the process, our challah dough, to rise.

Note to my reader: To the novice challah baker, yeast seems to be the scariest part of the process. I'm here to tell you, don't fear the yeast! Proofing the yeast will determine whether or not the yeast is working and, as long as conditions are right (very warm water and some sugar, see page 174 for more detailed instructions) the yeast will do its job and your challah will rise.

Did everything right and the dough still isn't rising? See RISING! (the cookbook,) for troubleshooting a non-rising dough.

Sugar vs. Salt
: the great debate

While sugar and salt may seem like simple flavor additives and extraneous to the essential building blocks of a challah dough, they are, in fact, quite necessary in the creation of a perfect challah.

Sugar and salt, while both crucial elements in the challah dough, serve opposite and even opposing functions. Sugar encourages the growth of yeast and the subsequent rising of the dough. Salt does the absolute inverse of this. It serves to quell the rising, inhibiting the growth of the dough and creating a tighter structure of gluten strands.

So herein lies the great debate: to sweeten or to brine? Would we create giant swelling mounds of yeasty goodness, or tightly controlled spheres of gluten correctness?

Of course, this debate doesn't end with dough. It always goes back to the nurture balance. So read on . . . *and decide for yourself!*

"WHATEVER WE ARE DOING, NO MATTER HOW
HOLY, WE SHOULD NEVER BE SO ENGROSSED
AS TO MISS THE SOUND OF A CHILDS CRY."

—Rabbi Schneur Zalman of Liadi
(the Alter Rebbe)

Sugar
: the first addition: infancy

Isn't it incredible that yeast needs sugar in order to grow?

So perfect.

How do we encourage healthy rising? We begin with sweetness.

In comparing the creation of a dough to a recipe for nurturing, the beginning of the dough process parallels infancy. Infancy, whether literal or emotional, is not a time for discipline. It is a time for pure sweetness and warmth.

When Babies Cry

As mentioned earlier, the first lesson we learn in life is that of trust and faith. It is the mother who is uniquely positioned to provide this first and most crucial life lesson. When a child cries and his cries are immediately answered, there is a deep understanding that resounds in the child's psyche: I am loved and cared for. My needs are important and I am heard.

Not everyone agrees with answering a baby's cries immediately. As a matter of fact, there is an entire contingency of parenting "experts" devoted to warning mothers of the dangers of spoiling their babies.

Remember your inner, quiet, persistent voice that knows the answer even when you think you don't? Well, mine told me to pick up my children as soon as they cried. And I am so grateful that I listened. Above the cacophony of voices telling me that I was ruining them, not allowing them to "self-soothe," and destroying their ability to ever fall asleep on their own.

They have grown up. They have no trouble sleeping through the night these days (waking them up in the morning is the much larger problem now!), they are exceptionally proficient at comforting themselves, and they feel completely loved and heard. I am so glad I was able to tune out all the opinions to the contrary.

Chasidic teaching and lore clearly promotes the prompt response to a child's cry. There is a famous story told of the Alter Rebbe, the great master, Rabbi Schneur Zalman of Liadi (the one from the "Shmuel Munkes story" on page 56), who lived in the apartment above his son, Rabbi Dovber.

> *In the deep of night, the Alter Rebbe, immersed in his studies, heard the loud and persistent cries of his infant grandson, a son of Reb Dovber, in the apartment below. As the minutes passed and the baby's cries went unanswered, the Alter Rebbe left his holy books and went down to the child. He picked up the child and comforted him, not leaving him until the child was fast asleep.*

Though the baby's father had been sitting near the child the entire time, he had been so deeply immersed in his holy books, he had not even heard the child's cry. When Reb Dovber finally became aware of his father's presence in the room, the Alter Rebbe rebuked him gently, saying, "One must never be so immersed in study or Divine service as not to hear the cry of a child in need."

There is nothing in the world more important than answering a child's cry.

There is a similar story told of Rabbi Moshe Leib of Sassov, the holy Sossover Rebbe.

While walking to synagogue one Yom Kippur eve, the Sossover Rebbe heard the cries of a child from within a home. When he realized that there was nobody there to comfort the child, he entered the home and rocked the child himself. The baby's mother had thought the child was asleep and had run to the synagogue to hear a bit of Kol Nidrei, the awesome opening prayers of Yom Kippur. Her child had, however, awoken scared and alone and the Sossover Rebbe would not leave him in that state. All those who had assembled in the synagogue waited in wonderment for their Rebbe to appear for Kol Nidrei. When the Rebbe finally did appear, he began the Kol Nidrei service with the reprimand that no child's cry should ever go unanswered.

The Need for Attention

One of my favorite *New Yorker* cartoons from over the years—in fact, one that I have deemed "fridge worthy," though, alas, I have forgotten the name of the artist who created it—goes like this:

There are two women seated on a couch drinking coffee, apparently trying in vain to have an adult conversation. Behind them, standing on the back of the couch, is a small child who is writing in huge letters on the wall, "I WANT ATTENTION!" "Oh, don't mind him," the mother says to her friend, "he just wants attention."

Have your laugh, but why is a child's need for attention any less urgent than his need for food? Indeed, giving him attention demonstrates that he matters to you. It means that his existence counts and that he is recognized in this world as being important. Attention is important! If a child cries and "just wants to be held," that is a valid need. A need that is as valid as the need for physical nourishment.

This brings me to today's trend of letting a baby cry it out, otherwise known as CIO (when you abbreviate it, it sounds scientific, doesn't it?). This is supposed to teach a child to "self-soothe" and develop healthy sleep patterns.

The *Early Human Development* journal published research conducted at the University of North Texas in August, 2011.[1] Observing 25 infants aged 4–10 months in a five-day inpatient sleep training program, researchers monitored levels of the stress hormone cortisol in the babies, who were left to cry themselves to sleep without being soothed.

---

[1] Middlemiss, Wendy et al. "Asynchrony of Mother–infant Hypothalamic–pituitary–adrenal Axis Activity following Extinction of Infant Crying Responses Induced during the Transition to Sleep." *Early Human Development* 88 (2012): 227-32. Http://anaesthetics.ukzn.ac.za/Libraries/Documents2011/Early_human_development_June12.sflb.ashx. Web. 16 Mar. 2015.

The scientists measured how long the infants cried each night before they fell asleep. The mothers sat in the next room and listened to their children cry but were not allowed to go in and comfort them.

By the third night, the babies were crying for a shorter period of time and falling asleep faster. (See? Sleep training works!) *However*, the cortisol levels measured in their saliva remained high, indicating that the infants were just as "stressed" as if they had continued to cry hysterically. So, while the infants' internal physiological distress levels had not changed, their outward displays of that stress were extinguished by sleep training. Simply put, they had trained themselves not to communicate their distress, understanding that it wouldn't be listened to. *(Hmm . . . maybe not such a great thing.)*

Attention=Trust=Self Confidence

In his book, *How Children Succeed: Grit, Curiosity, and the Hidden Power of Character,* Paul Tough examines the skills and traits that lead to success. Ultimately, he advances the hypothesis that character attributes may be more significant indicators of future success than cognitive skills such as IQ and intelligence.

"[I]n the past decade, and especially in the past few years," writes Tough, "a disparate congregation of economists, educators, psychologists, and neuroscientists have begun to produce evidence that . . . [w]hat matters most in a child's development . . . is not how much information we can stuff into her brain in the first few years. What matters, instead, is whether we are able to help her develop a very different set of qualities, a list that includes persistence, self-control, curiosity, conscientiousness, grit and self-confidence."

In other words, the bread of faith that is fed by the mother is the magic ingredient in the success of a human being.

In her article entitled "Dangers of 'Crying it Out,'" Darcia Narvaez, PhD writes, "With neuroscience, we can confirm what our ancestors took for granted, that letting babies get distressed is a practice that can damage children and their relational capacities in many ways for the long term. We know now that leaving babies to cry is a good way to make a less intelligent, less healthy but more anxious, uncooperative and alienated person who can pass the same or worse traits on to the next generation."

Dr. Narvaez goes on to cite research that has shown that babies left to cry alone in their cribs suffer from extreme distress and that the practice creates long-term effects, such as impaired growth and an inability to trust. Disturbingly, the neurons in the brain also wither away.

Developmental psychologist, Erik H. Erikson, famous for having coined the term "identity crisis," describes the first year of life as a sensitive period and a time for establishing a sense of trust in the world, which at that point is the world of the parent and the world of self. When a baby's needs are met without distress, the child learns that the world is a trustworthy place, that relationships are supportive, and that the self is a positive entity that can get its needs met. When a baby's needs are dismissed or ignored, the child develops a sense of mistrust of relationships and the world. In the process, self-confidence is undermined. The child may then very well spend a lifetime trying to fill the resulting inner emptiness.

Somehow, mothers have always known this instinctively: a mother's first reaction is always to respond to her child's cry.

It's only lately, since we've begun to ignore our own inner voices and listen to the "experts," that we've been denying what we know internally to be true.

Family Ties

My husband and I did not know each other until we met in our 20s but our families have had fascinatingly intersected histories. Our maternal grandfathers both came over on the same boat from Europe, arriving in Israel in 1948. Since then, there has been interconnectedness with the families that has transcended geographic location.

In the early '70s, when my older brother was a toddler and I was an infant, my parents had recently moved to Vancouver, BC, a remote outpost in those days, to start a Jewish community under the leadership and guidance of the Lubavitcher Rebbe. Times were tough and they lived in a tiny apartment with their two babies. It was at this time that my husband's maternal grandfather, a great and wise chasid known affectionately as Reb Avrohom Mayor (he originated from the town of Mayor, Russia), was traveling through the United States and Canada and arrived at my parents' home. My parents were honored by the presence of such an illustrious guest, but had no choice other than to place him in the one extra bedroom that they had, where their children slept, as well.

In the middle of the night, my mother woke my father frantically, telling him to pick up the crying baby (yup, that was me!) before the baby would awaken Reb Avrohom Mayor. My father quickly ran toward the bedroom but, when he got there, he realized that I had stopped crying. He tiptoed in to investigate and found the great chasid, Reb Avrohom Mayor, rocking me back to sleep. My father apologized profusely for having woken such a holy man, to which Reb Avrohom, whom I can now claim as my own grandfather and the namesake of my own baby, responded that *"m'lozt nisht a kind veinen,"* we don't allow a child to cry.

This is the way it has been done for centuries; this is how we raise a joyous and confident child. As my parents and grandparents knew from their parents, *"m'lozt nisht a kind veinen,"* we answer a child's cry. This is the bread of faith, the sustenance for a lifetime of kindness, nurturing, and self-acceptance.

Some of my earliest memories are of my paternal grandfather, himself a devoted chasid, brilliant in matters of mind and heart, rocking my baby siblings and cousins on his knee, singing in Yiddish, *"Du bist a zeese maydele [or yingale],"* you are the sweetest little girl (or little boy, depending on who was being held), melodiously infusing the child with an awareness of his or her inherent sweetness and goodness.

Infancy is not a time to "train a child;" it is the time for unconditional pouring of sweetness. The more sweetness, the more rising.

And this brings us back to our challah recipe—more specifically, to the sugar.

When observing the challah dough, this is obvious to us. We begin with a combination of water, living yeast, and sugar and we allow it to froth and start the rising process. If we can get this part of the recipe right, we're off to a great start! Adding salt at this point will kill the yeast and disrupt the rising process. Though the salt plays a crucial role in the challah recipe, it's all in the timing. Sugar first, salt later. We begin with sweetness and pure unconditional acceptance; discipline and boundaries will follow.

"A MAN SAID TO HIS AGENT,
'BRING A KOR OF WHEAT TO THE ATTIC FOR ME!'"
. AFTERWARDS, THE MAN SAID TO HIS AGENT, "DID YOU MIX INTO THE
WHEAT A KAV [MEASUREMENT] OF CHUMTON [**SALT**]?" "NO," SAID THE AGENT.
THE MAN SAID, "IT WOULD HAVE BEEN BETTER IF YOU HAD
NEVER BROUGHT THE WHEAT."

—A TALMUDIC PARABLE [SHABBAT 31A]

Love is a Boy,
by Poets styl'd,
Then Spare the Rod,
and spill [spoil] the Child.

—Samuel Butler, 1662

Salt

: in its time, in its measure

*The word **melach** (salt) is a compound of the word **m'lach** (from moisture).*

The punishing sun beats down on pure water and turns it into salt. While water represents life-giving *chesed*/kindness, salt represents the more restrictive *gevurah*/severity.

Gevurah is also understood as the energy of boundaries and discipline. Each creation in this world is an earthly manifestation of its spiritual source. Salt is not just an expression of gevurah. It is gevurah as we experience it in our physical reality.

While gevurah is seemingly a harsher and more difficult *sefirah*/expression than chesed, the paradox of gevurah is that it actually gives rise to chesed.

In his Kabbalistic treatise *Eitz Chaim*, Rabbi Chaim Vital[1] writes that gevurah on one plane creates chesed on the plane directly beneath it.

We see the way this manifests in our physical reality by the fact that, while salt on its own is gevurah, harsh and bitter tasting, when it is blended into another food, it becomes chesed, drawing out the sweetness of that food.

Salt is full of seeming contradictions. It can break down the most sturdy of stone and preserve the most tender of grain. In the Torah, G-d forms an everlasting covenant with Aharon, a *"covenant of salt" (Bamidbar 18:19)*. As Rashi[2] explains, *"G-d made a covenant with Aharon with something that is healthy, enduring, and preserves others. . .salt, which never spoils."*

Ages and Stages

The Jewish tradition is very cognizant of the fact that there are stages of children's development during which they must be left free and unrestrained, as well as times during which discipline must be introduced, although, even then, it is done gradually. As important as the initial sweetness and unbounded love may have been, boundaries and discipline—when used in the right measure and time—are equally essential in all of our nurturing, both of our loved ones and ourselves.

The age of three is traditionally considered to be the age during which one begins to discipline a child. This is symbolically demonstrated by giving the male child his first haircut at

1   *1542-1620; foremost disciple of Rabbi Yitzchak Luria, the Arizal*
2   *1040-1105; leading biblical commentator*

that time, trimming the wild, animalistic self that was allowed to grow, unfettered, during the first three years of his life.

Humans are likened to a tree of the field. The Torah's command that we allow all fruit trees to grow freely and untouched for their first three years demonstrates yet again that during the first three years of a child's life we are to withhold from harsh discipline.

Gevurah continues into life and is crucial in the way we nurture. In fact, it has been proven that a very strong indicator of future success in life is the ability to self-regulate and practice self-control. An individual's success in her 30s in terms of health, wealth, and more can be predicted by how well she can control her impulses as early as age three, says a recent study published in the *Proceedings of the National Academy of Sciences*.[3]

Salt on Top of Sugar

But salt, much like discipline, is a tricky thing. On its own, it is very bitter and even destructive. Yet, when added to an existing framework in measured amounts, it draws out the inherent sweetness that may otherwise have remained hidden. Used in large quantities, when appropriate, salt even preserves, keeping the framework intact.

The previous Lubavitcher Rebbe, Rabbi Yosef Yitzchak Schneerson, would tell a parable of one man who received exactly the same treatment from two different people, yet responded

---

3 *"A Gradient of Childhood Self-control Predicts Health, Wealth, and Public Safety." Proceedings of the National Academy of Sciences 108.7 (2011): 2693-698. Web.*

completely differently to each one of them.

> *Scenario 1: Sam is walking down the street, minding his own business, when, all of a sudden, Michael walks by with a bundle of sticks and starts lashing him. Sam is enraged and, as a result, begins to attack Michael. Suffice it to say, this story does not end well.*

> *Scenario 2: Sam enters the bathhouse for his weekly shvitz (sauna). He is brought into a warm, steamy room, where he is relaxed and massaged for the better part of an hour.*

> *Following this pampering session, Sam enters the treatment room, where Michael is waiting for him with a bundle of sticks. Michael proceeds to lash Sam violently with the sticks and Sam thanks him profusely for the wonderful therapy.*

Same lashing, completely different reaction. It's the warmth and sweetness that make all the difference.

When we need to impose discipline, boundaries, and gevurah in life, we need to first be sure that we have laid the groundwork of kindness, warmth, and acceptance. In this way, the gevurah will not only be accepted, but welcomed and transformative.

In the nurturing of ourselves, as well, while we propel ourselves forward always and do not allow ourselves complacency, the momentum needs to come from a place of deep acceptance and love.

The Strength in Salt

Salt is not only beneficial in the creation of a perfect challah dough – it is quite necessary. Salt actually tightens and strengthens the gluten structure and prevents an over-rising. This control of the level of yeast activity allows the dough to rise slowly, surely, and gradually, encouraging the full development of flavor.

Thus, the salt in our challah recipe is very similar to gevurah in the structure of our lives and our nurturing. It is not only beneficial, bringing out the inherent sweetness and flavors, it is completely necessary. In fact, without the proper usage of salt, or gevurah, we risk an over-rising, much like the inflammation of ego as previously discussed.

We live our lives striving for the balance of chesed and gevurah, sugar and salt.

Very often, homemade challah will be slightly bland, due to the common fear of over-using salt and killing the yeast and thus preventing a proper rising. I'm here to tell you that if you've created a conducive environment for rising, a nice blend of warmth and sweetness, you don't have to fear the salt!

Go ahead and be liberal with it; your challah is protected and will only be more delicious and successful for the addition of the extra salt. And, rest assured, it will rise.

Oil & Eggs

While challah can technically be made with nothing but flour and water, the addition of yeast, sugar, and salt will assist greatly with the rising process and add to the flavor profile.

The addition of the next two ingredients—oil and eggs—complete the basic building blocks of almost every challah recipe out there (except for, of course, vegan, fat-free, and gluten-free [which I will cover most thoroughly in the ***RISING!*** cookbook—something for everyone!]).

In all the ingredients that lead to the magical processes that happen in our kitchens everyday, oil and eggs stand out as particularly significant.

"YOU PREPARE A TABLE BEFORE ME IN THE PRESENCE OF MY ENEMIES;
YOU ANOINT MY HEAD WITH OIL; MY CUP OVERFLOWS."

—TEHILLIM 23:5

Oil

The Jewish tradition is rich with references to oil, particularly the wondrous olive oil, or EVOO as foodies have taken to calling it these days.

Every day it seems there are new scientific revelations regarding the benefits of olives and olive oil for health and wellbeing. Heart health, skin benefits, immunity-boosting powers, and anti-aging support are some of the most studied and widely cited applications of the fruit of the olive tree.

The olive fruit is unique in that each fruit is borne of two flowers. This seems to allude to the two life forces that enliven each of us –both the spiritual and the physical – which we must each possess for life to occur.

Oil itself is a unique substance. It spreads itself and moistens all it comes in contact with, imbuing all it touches with its richness, yet it always remains separate, distinct, retaining its unique characteristics.

RISING

There is a strong desire within us for sameness, to identify ourselves with our surroundings by recognizing the things we have in common. This is a very human characteristic, and a particularly feminine trait, as well.

Often referred to as the herd mentality, it seems we have a strong need to follow the direction of others, both male and female, of the human race. Professor Krause, with PhD student John Dyer, conducted a series of experiments[1] in which groups of people were asked to walk randomly around a large hall. Only a select few within the group received detailed information about where they were going. All those in the experiment were not allowed to communicate with each other and had to stay within arm's length of another person. The published findings showed that "In all cases, the informed individuals were followed by others in the crowd, forming a self-organizing, snake-like structure . . . . In large crowds of 200 or more, five percent of the group was enough to influence the direction in which it traveled."

In other words, we are often only following a select few and undervaluing our own perceptions, qualities, and capabilities, thinking that "other people" know better. In a world where "diversity" is the catchall phrase, we often, surprisingly, forget to honor our very own distinctiveness.

In nurturing others, and ourselves, we are charged with an awesome responsibility to acknowledge uniqueness as worthy of celebration.

The oil reminds us that by retaining our distinct characteristics, we have great potential to enrich our surroundings, bringing life and light to the world around us.

---

1   University of Leeds. "Sheep In Human Clothing: Scientists Reveal Our Flock Mentality." ScienceDaily. ScienceDaily, 16 February 2008.

Somehow, the opinions of friends, parents, school principals, well-meaning grandmothers in the grocery store, and the random guy at the checkout counter seem to crowd out our inherent knowledge of our uniqueness and that of the ones we love and nurture. When we find ourselves agreeing with their assessments, we need to take a step backwards and inwards and rediscover that which we already know about the ones we love—including ourselves. Namely, the things that make us individual and special are the very things that make us different from the people around us.

Love is a Mirror

The way we perceive our loved ones is the way they will see themselves.

We all have an innate desire, and incredible ability, to nurture others in a way that breathes life into them. The first messages we impart to those we mother are the ones that stick and follow them around as their inner voice for the rest of their lives. These messages are constantly "breathing" into their daily existence, adding positive energy and impetus if they were imparted positively and, unfortunately, potentially doing great harm if imparted negatively.

This process begins at birth.

Miri, a sweet new mom in my community, called me in tears only four weeks after the birth of her first child. "Rebbetzin, what do I do? My baby screams all day! He's only happy when being held close and rocked. When he's hungry, he shrieks like the world is coming to an end. When his diaper needs changing, you can think he's being tortured. I'm starting to think of him as difficult, moody, and unhappy. What do I do?"

I replied, "This is what you do: You take those words out of your vocabulary and out of your brain. When he screams like the world is coming to an end, you say to yourself and to your child, 'What a determined person this little boy is! He will not stand for mistreatment. He will make sure he gets what he needs in life. How lucky I am that I have a child who is so capable of expressing his needs and does not allow the world to overlook him. Look how he loves to be held; he is a loving, warm, and social person. He knows how to receive love and to accept the love I have to give him. How lucky I am to have such a loving person to nurture.'"

Say it out loud. Say it to anyone who will listen. You will believe it and they will believe it, and it will be the truth.

Every personality trait is positive if directed toward positivity, if viewed in the light of love and acceptance. When we view our screaming, seemingly unhappy baby as a person with great determination and stamina, not willing to take abuse, we empower her to be that person. And she will be that person and the world will see her as that person – a person to be admired and loved for those very qualities.

Not everyone is blessed to have had positive messages about their unique qualities breathed into them from the start. Most often, people spend their lives struggling against the negative messages about their very selves that they must overcome. But, we can all access these positive, life-affirming messages at any time in our lives simply by recognizing the purity and perfection of our inner core. We remember that at our essence we are a piece of the Divine and that that essence is a gift that is uniquely, incredibly, our own.

Immediately upon awakening, we greet the day with *Modeh Ani,* a short prayer that gives thanks to our Creator for the gift of a new day. We end with the words, *"raba emunatechah/*great is Your faith in us." The message is that if we are alive and on this earth today, it is because we have been entrusted with tremendous gifts to impart to this world and there is a deep faith from the One who gives life that we will indeed do so today.

We continue with the prayer, *"Elokai, neshamah shenatata bee, tehorah hee. Atah veratah, atah yetzartah, atah nefachtah bee/* My G-d, the soul that You have given me is pure and perfect. You created it, You formed it, and You breathed it into me."

Go forward into the day, and into the world, armed with the knowledge of your inherent perfection. If you deny it, you deny the very gifts you were given.

When we are sure of our own deep perfection, we will instinctively pass on this knowledge to all those we nurture. For if we are perfect as we are, so are they.

When you add the oil to your challah dough, watch how difficult it is to blend it into the mix. See how stubbornly it insists on remaining separate and distinct, and see how, when blended into your dough, the entirety of the dough becomes smoother, richer, and more beautiful.

Oil was used in ancient Judaic tradition to anoint the "chosen ones," kings and priests and prophets. Today we recognize that each one of us can be "chosen." We anoint our loved ones and ourselves, rising with this knowledge of our uniqueness.

"Probably one of the most private things in the world is an egg, until it is broken."

—MFK Fisher

Eggs

Now that we have spent all this time extolling the virtues of diversity and distinctiveness and what keeps each of us unique and separate, I want to digress and talk about the other side of the coin, or the egg as it were.

While oil stands apart, rises above, and retains its original characteristics throughout, eggs seem to do the exact opposite. Eggs are binding—the glue that holds our dough together. The eggs spread throughout the dough, taking the separated oil and water and creating an emulsion, bringing the dough together as a cohesive whole. While oil on its own will not mix with anything and will only disperse throughout the other liquids, when eggs are added, this changes.

As women, we are uniquely gifted with the ability to draw people together into family, community, and village. Deborah Tannen writes in her bestselling *You Just Don't Understand: Women and Men in Conversation* that women tend to see the world as a "network of connections," and that their communications and interpretations of others' communications seek to "preserve intimacy and avoid isolation."

With the recognition of our shared humanity and the innate ability to observe the similitude in all of creation, women become the glue that holds the world together.

Do you know what happens when eggs are heated? The egg proteins uncurl and bump into other proteins that have also uncurled and new chemical bonds form. However, rather than binding the protein to itself, these bonds connect one protein to another.

Eggs as an ingredient are interesting in that they are an embryonic form of life. It is the unique ability to form life, from its very embryonic stage, that defines the nurturing capability of the woman. In Kabbalistic terms, the male energy is that of *chochmah*, the initial spark of life that is placed into the vessel of *binah*, which contains the capacity to actualize that spark and nurture it into being. The child of this union is *daat*, a knowledge that is an intimate blend of the two, an actualization of both energies.

In the process of forming life, both on a biological level and on an emotional level, the woman is both the "blender" and the "egg itself." She takes all the random bits of information and inspiration, makes the connections, and creates something that is alive.

As we add the eggs to our dough, we imagine that our shared soul roots, humanity, and love are bringing all the disparate pieces together and creating a perfect circle of acceptance and wholeness.

Adding the Extras

Flour, water, sugar, yeast, salt, oil, and eggs are the basic building blocks of a challah dough.

And here's where you start to have fun!

Challah baking is about creating something alive, warm, and nurturing. It's about bringing your own brand of homemade love and intention to the table. So, now it's time for you to add in the elements that make the challah your own.

In my "classic recipe" on page 173, you will see that I offer the option of adding vanilla. I adore vanilla. I would spray it on myself as perfume and bathe in it if I didn't fear that my children would mistake me for baked goods. Vanilla added to challah makes the whole thing just a little more sweet, cakey, and wonderful and that's how I like it.

Throughout the recipe section of the *RISING!* cookbook, I offer suggestions for other tasty additions—sometimes savory, sometimes sweet—to enhance your challah. Go crazy or stay simple; either way, a challah that is baked with intention and love is a representation of your best self and will be received as such by all who partake of it.

The Challah Bowl
: where it all comes together

I write this in the lovely Catskills, looking out at a large grassy area filled with children and happy noise. I have been coming here with my children for the better part of twenty years, and it is here that I mixed my challah dough today, making do with a large, flat tin pan instead of my old trusty challah bowl that I've left at home back in Brooklyn.

It was here, while mixing, that I had my latest realization: It's not just the ingredients that make up the challah dough. The vessel that receives them and allows them to combine is significant, as well.

Bread has been mixed in bowls for thousands of years. Try mixing the ingredients on a flat surface and you will understand why. The water starts sliding away from the center, the eggs go runny all over the place, and the flour just sits there, inert. *As you can tell, challah baking in the Catskills has been a whole lot of fun!*

True, many recipes call for the dough to be turned out onto a flat surface for the kneading stage, but until it is a solid mass, ready for kneading, it really needs a vessel that is shaped like a bowl.

A bowl creates a linear sink force, which causes all objects, regardless of their distance to arrive at the center at the same time. No matter where the ingredients start off, when put into a bowl, they come together in the center to become something more than when they began.

Women contain a bowl within them, as well: the womb, which is the container of life. It receives all the necessary ingredients for life and nurtures them, creating independent life.

According to Kabbalah, the feminine energy is a vessel that receives. This receiving is not a passive energy, rather one that takes in in order to bring forth. This receiving is the work we do everyday on this earth. We take the raw materials of life, gather them into ourselves, and shape them into something wonderful. This is the challah bowl. And it is from here that we watch our challah rise.

RISING

No greater thing is created suddenly, any more
than a bunch of grapes or a fig.
If you tell me that you desire a fig. I answer you
that there must be time. Let it first blossom,
then bear fruit,
then ripen.
—Epictetus

Chapter VI
The Rising

"The nature of the soul is to rise."

—Reb Schneur Zalman of Liadi (Tanya, Chapter 19)

RISING

Washington State University's bread lab bakers think they may have solved the mystery of the large recent increase in gluten intolerance.[1]

Aside from those who have Celiac disease and really can't process the gluten in wheat, most people should have no problem with it. The main reason for the inability to digest gluten today is the lack of rising time in industrial bakeries. Most industrial bakers allot only a few minutes for rising, resulting in a dough in which the yeast and bacteria have not had have enough time to digest all the gluten in the flour and the gluten structure does not have time to develop and strengthen. This creates a bread with an incompleted gluten process that is difficult for most people's digestive system to handle.

The rising time is crucial. In order to promote a healthy rising, we need to take a step back and allow time to do its thing.

---

1   Philpott, Tom. "Could This Baker Solve the Gluten Mystery?" *Mother Jones.* N.p., 12 Feb. 2014. Web. 18 Mar. 2015.

Sometimes, we may find that our dough is too tough or too sticky, or just not coming together properly. However, when given time to rise, these problems mostly seem to resolve themselves.

There is a method of allowing the dough to come together on its own, before starting the kneading process, which many professional bread bakers swear by. This resting period, where the ingredients are allowed to just merge naturally, is called the *autolyse*. The autolyse is most commonly done with just the flour and water, allowing for better absorption of the flour, as well as helping the gluten and starches align. And then comes the hands-on (or machine) kneading process.

I like to think of this as a lesson in our own nurturing. There is a time for hands-on care, when we need to put our whole selves into the process, getting down into the trenches and "getting our hands dirty."

Then there is the wisdom of knowing when to take a step back. So many of the things we spend so much energy on, both physical and emotional, will resolve themselves if given the time and space to work themselves out.

I like to call this aspect of our caretaking "benign neglect." And, as my children have grown, I have come to appreciate this as a crucial aspect of nurturing.

When we leave our dough to rise, we make sure to put it in the most conducive environment, a place of warmth and moisture, yet we are also careful to allow it enough space to rise on its own, undisturbed. We don't forget about our dough but we go about our business, keeping an eye on it from a distance. We allow it to do its thing while looking out for anything out of the ordinary that may call for our gentle interference.

RISING

Sometimes, we notice that the dough isn't rising. It is then that we need to troubleshoot and figure out how to get it to grow to its full potential. At times, we see that it is rising too quickly and we need to punch it down to bring it back to its proper form.

Facilitating the rising process is an especially apropos metaphor for the adolescent stage. However, the act of stepping back and giving our children, or ourselves, some space to rise, is really something that applies throughout all our lives.

In child raising this begins in infancy. In the early years, it may be that parents are rushing their children to toilet-train, or pressuring them to act socially proper before they are really ready. In this case, as nurturers, they are putting their children in a situation for which they are not fully prepared and this can negatively affect their rising.

Allow them to be. This is the greatest wisdom.

In all our nurturing capacities, be it in friendship, marriage, or mentorship, this aspect of taking a step back to allow for rising is a deep and necessary truth. Oftentimes, we just feel like we want to do something. . . anything, when the most effective thing is simply to do nothing.

This does not mean disappearing and checking out. On the contrary, this is just like rising a challah dough.

We keep a watchful eye on the rising, establishing a conducive environment and checking in occasionally to ensure that all is well. Even a situation that calls for silence still requires our presence, be it physical or simply our presence of mind.

Try practicing benign neglect, or, to state it more positively, *emotional liberation*! Leave the dough alone. It will do its thing brilliantly. And you can watch from a distance with pride.

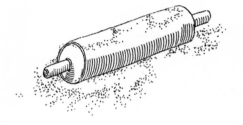

In his formation on the sixth day of creation, Adam's body was

"KNEADED [LIKE A DOUGH] FROM THE [EARTH OF THE] GROUND,"

(SANHEDRIN 38B)

into which G-d exhaled a Divine soul
to elevate and uplift him from a purely materialistic existence.

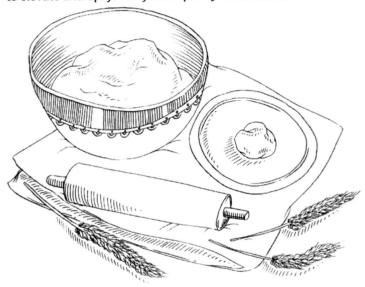

"ADAM IS THE CHALLAH OF THE WORLD."

(BEREISHIT RABBAH 14:1)

This indicates the humans' exalted status that relies on our ability
to elevate ourselves and the world around us
just as the portion of challah is sanctified to G-d.

Chapter VII

Hafrashat Challah,
Separating the Challah
: a Weekly Invitation to Reconnect

So, here we are! I'm glad you've made it this far.

We've come a long way on our challah journey. We've explored the idea of challah as a gift, revealed the joy of the process, reflected on the great female triad of challah, and discovered the recipe for challah as the perfect nurturing tutorial.

Now, I want to take you to the very beginning – before we ate challah, before we even ate bread – to when we were but newborns feeding off white manna "milk."

Let's travel a bit back in time, shall we, and discover how and where this challah thing began.

A Journey Ends, a Journey Begins

They are in the desert. All of them. The Israelites stand at the banks of the Jordan River, their miraculous journey of epic proportions about to culminate in its original purpose. All the pain and suffering of hundreds of years are coming to an end with their arrival to the land that has been gifted to them by G-d and will be for them and their children as an inheritance forever.

They are being handed this magical land of milk and honey on a giant proverbial silver platter. All that needs to be done is to step forward and enter. It is incredible.

They are terrified.

This journey was not just a geographical one, although there was a lot of that happening, too. It wasn't simply about traveling from Egypt to Israel. The Hebrews had evolved from a small tribe, to an enslaved people, to a ragtag bunch of escapees, and, somewhere along the way, to a nation. A family. A chosen people.

Having been given the Torah, they were now being entrusted to lead humanity in the marriage of heaven and earth. They were being thrust into the universal limelight where they would remain forever as a shining beacon, an example of the very best that humanity has to offer.

Their time in the desert was an oasis. Having just experienced the peak of Divine revelation, during which they received the wisdom that would guide them for all time, they were in a state of spiritual bliss. All their needs were being magically met and there were no worries as to sustenance, location, and bodily needs. The Jewish nation was fledgling, newborn, and cradled protectively in G-d's radiance.

This was all about to end. It was time to grow up.

The men were unhappy about this. It felt like a step down. Here, in the desert, they were cradled and protected and occupied only with lofty, spiritual matters. Now, they were tasked with entering a land they would need to conquer with their hands and then toil over, digging, planting, and reaping in its soil. It felt like dirty work and a descent from their exalted desert existence.

But the women understood.

Women are the first line of defense in nurturing and creating life. Producing and cultivating is messy work. So much of what is required in the nurturing endeavor is repetitive and mundane. But women hold within them an awareness of the intrinsic holiness camouflaged within the most earthly of tasks.

What the Women Know

After forty years of wandering, it was Yehoshua who was to lead the people into the land. Hoshea, as he was known then, needed this energy from the women who understood.

A small letter, a *Yud*, was added to his name. It was a gift to him by an ancestor long deceased: his foremother Sarah. Her name had been Sarai, but G-d had changed it to Sarah. The *Yud* that had been removed from her name was then gifted to Yehoshua, along with Sarah's deep sense of earthly awareness and ability to see beyond matter, qualities that would prove essential as he led the Jewish people into their new existence.

Sarah's tent was one of holiness, a place of light and truth. The three wonders of her tent – the cloud of glory resting above it, the candles that always remained lit within it, and the challah that stayed fresh from week to week – were representative of the fact that she was fully aligned and constantly connected with the Source of all life.

In her relationships, in her home, and in her nurturing, she located the Divine within the mundane. Sarah, as the representative of all women, understood, with a sensibility far beyond her time, that the greatest of light can be excavated from the deepest of the dirt.

As the fledgling nation stood on the precipice of their new reality, they were scared. They worried that in their association with the earth, they would lose their connection to heaven. They needn't have worried. Heaven was coming with them. The laws of the new land would keep the awareness of a Higher Presence with them at all times.

Of these new laws of the land, there was one that stood out. It was different than the others and would endure—through time, space, and the evolution of human spiritual awareness—it was the mitzvah of challah.

A Message for All Time

As mentioned earlier, while the word *mitzvah* is usually translated as "commandment," the etymology of the word also allows us to understand it as a Divine invitation to connect. Through the intentional *(and even unintentional!)* act of a mitzvah, we become aware of our continued and inherent connection to our higher self and our very Source.

Such is the mitzvah of challah.

"Vehaya b'achalchem milechem ha'aretz . . . . Raishit arisote-ichem challah tarimu terumah . . . ./[A]nd it will be when you eat from the bread of the land . . . the first of your dough shall be "challah," separated, and given as a gift" *(Bamidbar 15:19, 20).*

The next verse continues and states that this is a gift that will be separated for future generations, as well, creating a unique situation. Challah is a gift that continues to be given, wherever in the world we may be and whichever generation we find ourselves in.

The Challah Awareness

Some two thousand years ago, when our Temple stood, challah translated into a gift of dough for the priests in the Temple, whose sole occupation was the service of G-d. Giving them the first and best of our sustenance was our way of expressing recognition of the service they provided for the entire nation, keeping the connection of the Jewish people to the spiritual alive and present.

Today, we have evolved into a "Sarah," or feminine, awareness of the inherent Divinity in all of creation. Our home has become our temple, we ourselves are the priests in service of the Divine, and the Shabbat table is the altar upon which we place the challah. The separation of the challah, the sanctified piece of dough taken from the whole, is a powerful statement of our awareness of the Source of our sustenance.

Separating challah is one of the most powerful ways through which to give *tzedakah*. Tzedakah, often incorrectly translated as charity, means justice. When we give of our own sustenance, we are not doing something that is unusual and out of the ordinary out of the kindness of our hearts; we are simply doing justice in the system of giving and receiving that is the foundation of a balanced universe.

Throughout the week, we are in an active "creation" mode, making things happen with our minds and our bodies. As we make our challah on Friday, we begin the shift into a "being/gratitude" reality. In the separating of the challah we begin ushering in the day of Shabbat with the active recognition of the Source of all our blessings and sustenance.

Challah is a gift, the gift of gratitude and awareness of a higher, ethereal reality that is the source of all we have. In a world that is simply matter, particles, atoms, and neutrons, there is no space for this awareness. However, in a world that recognizes all physical matter as being but a reflection, or manifestation, of a transcendent reality, acknowledging the Source of our sustenance by removing a piece of dough that was intended for our own survival is completely natural.

With the separation of the piece of challah, we remember our essential immortality and our connection with the Infinite light and potential.

Reaching into Transcendence

In a world of mere particles, cause and effect is king. It is an "if... then" reality. *If* a doctor tells a patient that, G-d forbid, the patient has weeks to live, *then* the person will indeed not live much longer. *If* we put seeds into the ground and it rains, *then* the plants will grow; otherwise, they will wither. *If* we go to work each day, *then* we will make the amount of money we have been promised in our contract agreements, no more and no less.

But we are not mere particles. Cause and effect are only our reality when we are tied closely to our dense, material form. There is a spark of life within each of us, and every creation that has ever existed, that is eternal. It is the *nishmat chaim*, the breath of life that is breathed into us from the Source of all life. We call it our soul. It is the core of our very existence and our link to eternity.

In removing the piece of challah from our dough, we are reestablishing our connection with the part of ourselves that transcends our bodily form. We are linking to our infinite, formless selves and, as such, tapping into the pool of all possibility.

When we reach into that space, we remember that everything is possible.

This is the space from which we pray. As we recite the blessing upon separating the challah, we are reaching the space of infinite possibility – the Source of all blessings.

Making Miracles Happen

We start with the words *"Baruch atah,"* which mean "You are the Source of blessing," and the *breicha*, the reservoir from which all blessings flow. From that place we connect to the nameless, *"Atah/* You," the Unity of all that exists, and draw it down until we say the words, *"lehafrish challah/*to separate the challah," when the very blessing becomes embodied within the physical act of pulling off a piece of dough.

After reciting the blessing, we remove a piece of dough. We then hold that piece of dough and say, *"Harei zu challah/*Behold, this is challah."

The very declaration makes it so. *"G-d spoke and the world came into being."* Speech creates reality. By verbalizing aloud that this is challah, we acknowledge the sacredness, the otherness, of this piece of dough; it is no longer the same as the rest of the dough and, as we hold it in our hand, feels like the featherweight of eternity.

This deeply meditative and prayerful time is an incredible opportunity to reconnect to our deepest, truest self on a weekly basis and I highly recommend it.

We hear of many miracles that occur as a result of these deeply connective moments. A quick caveat here: I am not a "miracle" person per se, by which I really mean that magic tricks annoy me. I like to see the logic of all things. I was never so uncomfortable as when I sat through David Copperfield's magic hoopla—that stuff drives me crazy. Yet, I have seen countless stories happen before my eyes and I know that they are direct results of the incredible connection that can occur through the mitzvah of challah.

I have many of my challah students begging me to put miracle stories in here. I don't want to do that – but not because I haven't seen them. I have. They happened. Babies were created and birthed, people were healed, and love was found—and I saw it happen directly from the challah. And yet, I hesitate to enumerate the stories, because it feels too much like "abracadabra."

Challah is magical but we do not separate challah to perform a magic trick. We separate challah because it is a mitzvah and it brings us to a place of connectedness. What can happen from that place of connection is truly magical. But it is not a trick. It's simply a profound time when we connect to infinite potential and recognize our constant, eternal bond to that place.

What happens afterwards, well . . . maybe you'll send me your stories. I can add them to my collection. And, one day, who knows? Maybe I will write them down in a book, but I have to sit comfortably through a whole magic show first; I've seen bigger miracles happen.

Separating Challah
: a History

Challah, the separation of a portion of dough to be gifted to the kohen, is among the Torah commandments that are categorized as *t'luyot ba'aretz*/directly connected with the physical Land of Israel.

The Torah states: *"Vehaya b'achalchem milechem ha'aretz . . . . Raishit arisoteichem challah tarimu terumah . . . ."* [A]nd it will be when you eat from the bread of the land . . . the first of your dough shall be "challah," separated, and given as a gift *(Bamidbar 15:19, 20).*

This challah gift is among the twenty-four gifts that we were directed to give to the kohanim, the priests who served in the *Beit Hamikdash*/Holy Temple.

Some other *mitzvot* that are *t'luyot ba'aretz* include *bikkurim*, *terumah*, and *ma'aser*. *Bikkurim*/the First Fruits, were brought to Jerusalem by the landowner as an offering in the Temple and given to the kohanim. *Terumah* and *ma'aser*, portions of produce, were given respectively to a kohen and a Levite.

These other mitzvot were not applicable until fourteen years after the Israelites entered the land (seven years to conquer it and seven years to divide it amongst the tribes). However the mitzvah to take challah applied from the moment that the Israelites crossed the Jordan River into the promised Land.

By Torah law, challah is taken only within the boundaries of the Land of Israel. However, the sages instituted the taking of challah outside the Holy Land so that people living in the Diaspora would not forget the mitzvah.

In order for the mitzvah of challah to have the force of a *mitzvah d'oraita*/a Biblical commandment, all (or a majority, according to the Sefer HaChinuch) of Jews must be living in Israel. Ever since the forced dispersion of the Jews at the end of the First Temple era, this criterion has not been met. Therefore, challah today, both inside and outside of the Land of Israel, is a rabbinic rather than a Biblical mitzvah.

The word challah, though used to connote the bread we eat on Shabbat, is really the word for the piece of dough that is separated and given to the kohen, or, in our day and age, burned to be rendered inedible. This can be confusing, as the piece that is separated is actually dough, not the baked challah. Yet it is called "challah" as per the directive in the Torah.

The Laws of Hafrashat Challah
: a Digest[1]

The grains upon which a blessing and separation of challah is required:

Wheat, barley, oat, spelt, and rye. These are also the only grains from which a bread that requires the blessing of Hamotzi can be made.

Who may separate challah?

The mitzvah of challah separation applies to any Jew over the age of bar or bat mitzvah who makes a dough that meets the requirements for separation (see below). However, this mitzvah has become known as one that is specifically woman-centric and one of the three mitzvot unique to women. As part of her preparation of food for her family, the mitzvah of challah becomes symbolic of the practice of keeping kosher, a practice in which the woman of the house plays a pivotal role. If there is no woman available to separate the challah, a man may perform this mitzvah. If, however, a man and woman are both available, the mitzvah should be performed by the woman.

---

1 *For a complete overview of the laws of hafrashat challah (the separation of challah), please see* Kitzur Shulchan Aruch, *Chapter 35.*

Flour requirements for separation of challah

- Less than 2 lb. 11 oz. (1230 grams) of flour: *no separation of challah is required.*
- Between 2 lb. 11 oz. and 3 lb. 11 oz. (1666.6 grams) of flour: *challah is to be separated but without reciting the blessing.*
- Over 3 lb. 11 oz. of flour: *challah is separated with a blessing.*

Liquid requirements for separation of challah

To separate challah with a blessing, the majority of the liquid content must be water.

If the majority of the liquid is not water (i.e. honey, oil, eggs, milk, juice, etc.), challah is to be separated without a blessing so long as there is at least one drop of water in the dough.

Burning the challah piece

The piece of challah that was separated should be burned until it is rendered inedible. It should be wrapped in aluminum foil, or the like, and may then be burned in your oven or in any fire. However, the challah should not be burned while anything else is being baked in that oven.

Once the piece of challah has been burnt, it should be discarded but does not need to be disposed of in any particular manner.

If it is not possible to burn the piece of dough, it is also acceptable to discard it in the garbage. Care should, however, be taken to ensure that the piece of dough is properly wrapped—preferably double-wrapped—so that it doesn't come in contact with anything else in the trash.

Combining Doughs

If you are simultaneously making multiple doughs that are each too small to require challah separation (such as if your mixer is too small to contain a large batch of dough and you are therefore making multiples of the same recipe), the doughs may be combined once kneaded to allow for the separation of challah. Simply place all the small doughs into one container and cover the container with a cloth. Separate the challah from one of the dough pieces and make the blessing as usual.

If, however, you are making many small doughs at once but they will each be baked in another person's oven (such as if a group of friends gather to bake challah together but each participant makes a small batch of dough and will take it home to bake), the doughs cannot be combined to separate challah with a blessing.

Separating the challah after baking

If one forgot to separate challah before baking the dough, or the dough was too "runny" to separate while it was raw (such as in a gluten-free oat challah batter), or one baked cakes that require challah separation, challah may (and should) still be separated after baking.

Combine all the baked challahs or cakes together in a container and cover them with a cloth. Remove a small piece from one of the loaves and make the blessing as usual.

If one forgot to separate challah on Friday and only realized once Shabbat began, the challah may still be eaten on Shabbat, provided that this took place outside of the Land of Israel. A slice of the challah loaf from which challah can be separated after Shabbat should be set aside. This slice should be large enough for the challah to be separated from it while still leaving over a portion of challah to be eaten thereafter.

Separating challah from dough that is not being used for bread

For large quantities of cakes, cookies, and desserts that meet the requirements for challah separation, the laws of separating challah apply. However, since the water content in baked goods is generally the minority of the liquid, challah should be separated without a blessing.

When the dough is intended for cooking or frying (rather than baking), such as donuts or dumplings, challah should be separated without a blessing. However, if even a small portion of the larger dough will be baked, a blessing may be made over the separation.

RISING

A VISUAL GUIDE TO THE
CHALLAH SEPARATION REQUIREMENTS:

THE GRAINS UPON WHICH A BLESSING AND SEPARATION OF CHALLAH IS REQUIRED.

These are also the only grains from which a bread that requires the blessing of hamotzi is made.

BARLEY
WHEAT
RYE
SPELT
OAT

FLOUR

THE AMOUNT OF FLOUR THAT IS REQUIRED FOR SEPARATION OF CHALLAH.

There are three categories in the separation of challah:
1. Separation with a blessing
2. Separation without a blessing
3. No separation required at all

3 LB. 11OZ / 1666.6 GRAMS

1. When using *the above amount or more*, challah is separated with a blessing.

2. *In between the bottom and top amounts* requires separation of challah without a blessing.

2 LB. 11OZ / 1230 GRAMS

3. If using *less than the above amount* of flour no separation of challah is required.

The Blessing of Challah[1]

---

1 *For meditations and intentions during the blessing please see meditations beginning on page 155*

Separate a portion of dough—challah—from dough that has been made with at least one of these five grains: wheat, barley, oat, spelt, and rye. Separate it after the dough has been kneaded but while the dough is still whole, before dividing and shaping into loaves. (See page 128 for a digest of all details pertaining to this mitzvah.) Before separating the piece of dough, recite the following blessing:

בָּרוּךְ אַתָּה יְיָ אֱלֹהֵינוּ מֶלֶךְ הָעוֹלָם
אֲשֶׁר קִדְּשָׁנוּ בְּמִצְוֹתָיו וְצִוָּנוּ לְהַפְרִישׁ חַלָּה.

Ba-ruch A-tah A-do-nai Elo-heinu Me-lech ha-o-lam a-sher kid-sha-nu b'mitz-vo-tav v'tzi-va-nu l'haf-rish challah.

You, Ado-nai, are the Source of all blessings, our G-d, Master of the universe, who has sanctified us with His commandments and commanded us to separate challah.

Then, remove a small piece, approximately one ounce, from the dough. Immediately after doing so, hold the piece of dough aloft and say:

הֲרֵי זוּ חַלָּה.

Ha-rei zu challah.
Behold, this is challah.

Since we cannot give the challah to the kohanim and since we may not use it ourselves, the prevailing custom is to burn the piece of dough. It can be burned in the oven (or by any other means), though not while other foods are baking in it.[1]

If a person forgot to separate challah before baking, the challah may (and should) still be separated afterwards.[2]

For meditations and intentions on topics such as stillness, family, and generosity while separating the challah, please see "Challah Meditations" in this volume, on page 155.

---

[1] For more details on how to dispose of the challah piece, see above in the digest of laws, page 129.

[2] For detailed instructions on separating after baking please see page 130.

Chapter VIII

Challah Customs & Segulot

: Through the Generations and Around the Globe

RISING

Bread as a staple of family and community life, knows no cultural bounds.

Across nearly every race, country, and religion, bread is seen as a peace offering, a way of bringing people together, and is used in countless religious ceremonies. In Judaism, bread is more than just a physically nourishing staple: when it is baked as challah, it becomes the cornerstone of multitudes of traditions and rituals.

As challah is so profoundly significant to Jewish life, many customs and omens have developed around the making and separating of the dough, and the baking, serving, slicing, eating, and even disposing, of the challah itself in the thousands of years since the original Divine directive to separate the first of our dough, the challah, upon entering the Promised Land.

In the section that follows, I will share a number of these customs and their origins with you. Since many of these have been established as *minhagei yisrael*/Jewish tradition, they have taken on a holiness and intrinsic value in their observance. Some of these customs involve the shape of the challah, some concern the serving and disposing of challah, and still others are simply ideas that surround the separating of challah and its significance.

Perhaps, in your personal journey of challah baking, you will even create some new traditions of your own, which you can then pass down to the next generation of challah bakers!

SHAPES OF CHALLAH

There are many customs, mostly influenced by region, which call for special shapes of challah coinciding with Shabbat and other holidays in the calendar.

Braided Challah

The most common shape of challah as we know it today is the braided challah, and, more specifically, the six-braided challah. This tradition began in the fifteenth century. Interestingly, this coincided with the emergence of Kabbalistic wisdom into mainstream Judaism.

The significance of the six strands were explained by Kabbalists as follows:

a] The six strands represent the days of the week, the work days that are characterized by the separations of physical reality, or what we call the "Tree of Knowledge" reality. The braiding of those six strands into one perfect whole represents the weekday separations merging into the perfect whole of Shabbat, or the unified "Tree of Life" reality.

b] Two braided challahs of six strands each combine to equal a total of 12 strands, representing the 12 Tribes of Israel and the inclusion of all of them in our Shabbat celebration. This concept traces back to the *Beit Hamikdash*, in which there were always twelve showbreads, the *Lechem Hapanim*, which represented the Twelve Tribes.

c] There is a custom from the Arizal[1], sourced in his *piyyut/* liturgical poem, *"Azamer Bishvachin,"* that is traditionally sung during the Friday night meal. The Arizal writes, *"Shechinta titattar beshit nahami listar/*May the Shechinah be adorned by the six loaves on each side." Some fulfill this statement by placing six round challahs on their Shabbat table, while others use two six-strand challahs side by side, thereby achieving the six on each side.

Of course, the six-braided challah is also quite beautiful and unique and, as such, enhances our Shabbat observance. There are also other reasons attributed to the braided shape. There are those who claim that this is borrowed culture; there were other traditions of specially braided breads in fifteenth-century Europe and this may have influenced the braided challah shape as we know it today.

In the section below, where I speak about customs of serving and disposing of challah, I mention that there are many traditions surrounding the cutting of the chal-

---

1 *Rabbi Isaac (ben Solomon) Luria Ashkenazi (1534 - 1572.) A great sage and mystic, known as the holy "Ari/lion," he is considered the father of contemporary Kabbalah and his teachings are referred to as Lurianic Kabbalah.*

lah bread and that many are careful not to put a knife to their challah. The braided shape may have evolved to create convenient "tear-away" pieces that could be removed without needing a knife.

The braided challah strand can range from three strands to 12 strands and vary greatly in complexity. Of course, the six-braid strand is the most traditional and authentic to Kabbalistic tradition.

In the braiding section of the book on page 178, I will demonstrate for you the traditional six-braid challah. For more varieties of braiding techniques, see my cookbook, *RISING! The Book of Challah.*

Round Flat Challah

Sephardic Jews have no tradition of using a braided loaf. Instead, the Middle Eastern and Spanish-Portuguese communities, dating from the second century CE, would make a soft flat bread resembling the pita that we are familiar with today. In some traditions, twelve of these round challahs are used, representing the Lechem Hapanim. They are arranged in two layers of six breads with the central two challahs of the upper layer used for the Hamotzi blessing.

Depending on the region of origin, these soft round challahs varied in ingredients, texture, appearance, and size. The Moroccan Jews woud make a laffa-like challah while the Yemenite Jews had the tradition of both a *lachuch*, similar to a large crepe or pancake, and the flat round pita-like challah, called *saluf*, which is similar to a pita, but is slightly roasted and crispy on top.

Mizrachis of Central Asian-Bukharian descent use a bread called *leposhka*. Somewhat smaller in size than the lachuch or pita, it is also a flattish round disc, often with intricate dotted designs pierced into the center.

The Iraqi challah, probably most similar to the original show-breads of Temple times, is a round, almost flat, matzah-like bread, which is shaped over a pot cover and baked in a clay oven.

Round Raised Challah

A universally practiced tradition is that of using round chal-lahs on Rosh Hashanah, and, in some communities, throughout the entire month of Tishrei, in which the New Year and High Hol-idays are celebrated. The round shape signifies the cycle of life: just as in a circle there is no set starting point or ending point, so, too, in life, every moment can be utilized as a "start over" moment; we are always afforded the opportunity to begin anew.

Another way of interpreting the classic spiral Rosh Hashanah challah is that it represents the passage of time and our own growth and movement within that cycle of time.

We can view the forward march of time as both linear and cy-clical. This is represented in the spiral challah – the long strand for linear time rolled into a round shape for cyclical time. While time is always moving forward, it is also cyclical: "what goes around, comes around." The sun rises and sets, the seasons re-turn, and, each year, Rosh Hashanah arrives once again, signify-ing the beginning of a new year and an opportunity to re-experi-ence the energy of last year's Rosh Hashanah, but from a deeper and more evolved place.

When we combine the concepts of linear and cyclical time, we essentially create a "spiral" of time. While the cycle is repeating itself, each time it grows outwards as it grows upwards. Even though we are going through the same cycle every year, each time we experience the energy of Rosh Hashanah, and, indeed, all other high points in the year, we are afforded the opportunity to experience them from a more expanded and mature perspective.

Some have the practice of increasing the sweetness of the round Rosh Hashanah challah by adding raisins or honey to the dough, signifying our wish for a sweet year.

Challah Free-Form Shapes

LADDER CHALLAH: There is an Eastern European custom to make the challah in the shape of a ladder for Shavuot, the holiday in which we celebrate the giving of the Torah. The word ladder in Hebrew is *sulam*, which has the numeric value of 130, as does the word Sinai. The five rungs on the ladder represent the five books of the Written Torah. Some communities have the tradition of creating a ladder-shaped challah for Rosh Hashanah or the pre-Yom Kippur meal, to illustrate the ascent of our prayers towards heaven.

BIRD CHALLAH: The earliest known appearance of this challah was in eighteenth-century Ukraine, where it was made for the *Seudat Hamafseket*, the final meal before Yom Kippur. The challah is either formed in the shape of a bird, or as a small piece of dough perched atop the larger spiral to represent the bird. The bird is representative of G-d's protection, as is promised by the prophet Yeshayahu, *"Like flying birds, so shall the L-rd of Hosts protect Jerusalem, protecting and saving, passing over and rescuing"* (Yeshayahu 31:5).

HAND CHALLAH: Another custom from eighteenth-century Ukraine: the challah is formed into the shape of a hand for Hoshanah Rabah, the seventh day of Sukkot. This is the final day of teshuvah, when we ask for deliverance. The shape of the hand is meant to evoke our reaching out toward G-d for salvation and our receiving of His judgments and blessings.

Challah Shaped into Hebrew Letters

Jewish mystics in the eighteenth century in Safed, Israel sometimes baked challah in the shape of the Hebrew characters representing the number twelve: a *Yud* and a *Bet*.

According to Kabbalistic tradition each long challah is a line, representing a *Vav*, the letter that equals six. The numerical value of the two challahs together then equals twelve, the number of showbreads and Tribes of Israel.

OTHER CHALLAH TRADITIONS

How Many Challahs?

We recite the Hamotzi blessing over two challahs at our Shabbat or holiday table to symbolize the double portion of manna that fell each Friday while the Jewish people traveled through the desert. This reawakens our awareness of G-d as the Source of our sustenance. The two challahs also signify the two aspects of Shabbat as defined in the Torah: *shamor* and *zachor*, to keep it and to remember it.

Reb Mendel of Rimanov instructed his students to eat seven pieces of challah. While eating each piece, they were to have in mind that it corresponded to another day of the week. Doing so would draw the blessing of challah into each weekday.

Prayers and Verses to Recite

According to the Ben Ish Chai, the woman of the house recites the following verse as she places the challahs on the Shabbat table:

"This is the table that is before G-d" (Ezekiel 41:22).

It is also traditional to continuously recite the words *"l'kavod Shabbat kodesh/*in honor of the holy Shabbat" throughout the preparing, kneading, and braiding of the challah dough. This helps the baker keep his or her intentions pure and focused throughout the process.

Serving the Challah

There is a tradition to throw a piece of challah, once it has been cut, toward each person seated around the table. There are various explanations for this tradition: The Sephardic tradition interprets this action as representing a downpour of wealth and sustenance, since challah represents our livelihood and nourishment. The Ashkenazi tradition ascribes this custom to the idea that handing another person bread is akin to giving him a hand-out and indicates a state of poverty. As such, Ashkenazim are careful not to put the challah directly into the recipient's hands and merely toss it toward the center of the table or toward each person at the table.

Disposing of Challah

There are various traditions regarding the disposal of chal-lah, since the challah takes on a form of holiness in its use for a mitzvah. Some communities are particularly vigilant in their adherence to this custom. They will not throw away any challah; instead they feed the leftovers to the birds. Others are simply careful to dispose of challah in a respectful manner by not al-lowing any large pieces to be thrown away and by wrapping the challah before disposing of it.

Dipping the Challah into Salt

The prevailing custom is to dip the challah (in fact, all bread) into salt before eating the first bite.

Our homes are our temples and our tables, the altar. On the original altar, there was always a quantity of salt. So, too, we make sure to keep salt on our table for each meal with bread *(Berachot 55)*.

Many communities have the tradition to dip their bread into the salt three times. The source of this tradition is a numerical one. The word *melach*/salt, is the word *lechem*/bread, read in reverse. The numerical value of both those words is 78, which is three times 26, the numerical value of G-d's name (the Tetragrammaton), the name that represents chesed, pure giving. Thus, dipping the *lechem* into *melach* three times is a way to draw in chesed and sweeten judgments.

Additionally, the word *mazlah* (the mazal) has a numerical value of 78. By dipping the bread into salt, we are symbolically bringing good *mazal*/luck into our lives.

Tearing vs. Cutting

Since our tables are compared to the altar and there were no knives or metal objects of any kind permitted upon the altar, some communities are careful not to put a knife to their challah and tear it instead. Some claim that this is actually where the tradition of braiding challah began, since it created a bread loaf with pieces that could easily be torn off. Another reason for avoiding the use of a knife on challah is that knives represent destruction and challah represents healing and wholeness.

Interestingly, though, there is also a well known custom to mark the challah that will be used first, prior to tearing or cutting into it. This marking is usually done with a knife. The challah that will be cut into first is marked slightly, and then the challahs are both lifted for the recitation of the blessing upon them. When they are being held for the blessing, they are held side by side, with the right challah slightly lower than the left. There is a tradition to cut the bottom challah first on Friday night and the top challah first on Shabbat day. This stems from the Kabbalistic teaching that the feminine expression of Divine energy is dominant during the first part of Shabbat, on Friday eve, and the masculine energy in the second part, on Shabbat day.[2]

---

2   *The Shulchan Aruch and the Ramah write that on Friday night the bottom chal-*

RISING

Covering the Challah

Across all communities and traditions, there is a custom to cover the challah on the Shabbat table before kiddush is recited. The simple explanation for this custom is that we don't wish to shame the challah by giving the kiddush wine precedence in its presence. In Jewish tradition, bread takes precedence over all other foods, even wine.[3] However, on Shabbat we recite kiddush over wine before making the blessing on the challah. As such, the challah is covered so as not to cause it the pain of embarrassment.[4] This is meant to be a tremendous lesson in sensitivity for us at the Shabbat table. If we are so careful not to embarrass a loaf of bread, how careful must we be with the feelings of those surrounding us at our table.

There is also a tradition for the challah to be set between two protective layers—a covering on top of them and a cloth or board beneath them—representing the two layers of dew, one above and one below, that protected the manna.[5]

---

lah should be cut first, since the bottom challah represents the feminine and on Shabbat eve, Shabbat is referred to as "Shabbat Queen" (Orach Chaim 274:1 Magen Avraham.). This is consistent with Kabbalistic tradition. Others write to cut the top challah first on Friday night (Kol Bo, Mitzvah 24).

3   Jewish law stipulates that the blessing over bread is always to be recited first and in favor of the blessings over all the other foods to be eaten at the same meal.

4   Tur, Orach Chaim 271

5   Tosefos, Pesachim 100b. Taz, Orach Chaim 271:12

CHALLAH SEGULOT

- Separating the challah is a powerful time for personal prayer. The name Chana is commonly taught as an acronym for the three special mitzvot of women: *challah*, *niddah*/family purity, and *hadlakat hanerot*/Shabbat candles.

  Historically, Chana was the antecessor of the system of prayer as we know it today, representing effective communication with the Divine. Through the three mitzvot that make up her name—separating challah, renewing ourselves in the mikvah, and lighting Shabbat candles to illuminate our environment—we are able to similarly connect and communicate with our higher selves and our Source.

- The following custom has recently become common among Jewish communities: Forty[6] women devote their prayers while separating challah to the merit of a person in need of salvation (such as recovery from illness, a worthy mate, or the birth of a child). Some say this should be done with a group of 43 women.[7]

- The mitzvah of separating challah is recognized as a segulah for an easy, safe birth. It is customary for a woman to separate challah at least once in the ninth month of pregnancy.[8]

---

6   *The number 40 is significant in terms of radical change from one capacity to another, such as the 40 se'ah measurement required for a mikvah, the body of water that transitions a person from one state of being into another, to be kosher.*

7   *The number 43 is the numeric value of the word challah. It is also the numeric value of the word gam (also), indicating a completion and inclusion. As such, it is a very significant number in terms of finding one's soul-mate.*

8   *Mishna Shabbat 2:6- Women may be judged during childbirth according to their observance of the three mitzvot of women.*

- According to our sages, the mitzvah of separating challah brings a blessing for prosperous livelihood into the home. "You shall give the first yield of your dough to the kohen to make a blessing rest upon your home" *(Yechezkel 44:30)*.

  An early German and Central European name for challah was *barches*, an acronym for the phrase *"Birkat Hashem hee taasheer*/Hashem's blessing brings riches"*(Mishlei 10:22)*.

  Another name for challah that relates to this verse, used in the same part of the world, is *dacher*.

- **Schlissel Challah:** A very popular tradition related to challah, this takes place only once a year, on the first Shabbat immediately following Passover. It is a tradition that relates to sustenance and there are various explanations given as to why this is done. The name given to this tradition is *"Schlissel Challah,"* or "Key Challah" and the custom is to either bake a key into the challah, make a key shape with dough on top of the challah, and some even form the entire challah in the shape of the key. The premise of this custom is that this particular Shabbat is an auspicious time for sustenance prayers, and the key on or in the challah represents the opening of the gates of sustenance for the coming year.[9]

---

9   *The earliest recorded source for this custom seems to be the sefer* Oheiv Yisrael *by Rabbi Avraham Yehoshua Heshel, the Apter Rav. He refers to the custom of schlissel challah as "an ancient custom," and offers numerous Kabbalistic interpretations for this custom. The Apter Rav writes that after forty years in the desert, the Jewish nation continued to eat the manna until the first Passover in the Land of Israel. They brought the Omer offering on the second day of Passover and from that day on, they no longer ate manna, but food that had grown in the Land of Israel. Since this time of year is when they began to concern themselves over their sustenance rather than having it fall from the sky each morning, the key on the challah is a form of prayer to G-d to open up the gates of livelihood.*

Another source for this custom is from the second mishnah in tractate Rosh

- Because of the tremendous *zechut*/merit that is attributed to the mitzvah of separating challah, it is recommended to bake challah, primarily for the purpose of fulfilling this mitzvah, at least once a year. Ideally, one should separate challah during the Ten Days of Repentance.[10]

- Our sages instituted that we perform the mitzvah of hafrashat challah outside of the Land of Israel so that we do not forget "the Torah of challah."[11] It follows, therefore, that performing the mitzvah of challah is a special segulah for remembering and improving memory.

- Challah is a special segulah for teshuvah in general and, even more specifically, for the *baal teshuvah*/returnee or a convert to Judaism.

This is because even wheat that was imported into the Land of Israel was considered to be wheat of the Holy Land. Therefore, we were required to take challah from it even at the time when challah was only separated from wheat of the Land of Israel. This is indicative of the possibility and the power of

---

Hashanah, which says that on Pesach we are judged on the grains, representing parnasah/livelihood. Rabbeinu Nissim asks, "If we are judged on Rosh Hashanah how are we then judged on Pesach?" He answers that on Pesach it is determined how much grain the world will have during the coming year, but on Rosh Hashanah it is decided how much of that grain each individual will receive.

The Meiri, however, says that on Rosh Hashanah it is decided whether one will live or die, suffer or live in peace, etc., but that Pesach is when we are judged with regard to the grains. Based on this there are a number of customs that are practiced by Sephardic communities on the night that Pesach ends, signifying our desire to be granted ample sustenance. In Syria and Turkey they would put wheat kernels in all four corners of the house as a sign of prosperity for the coming year (Moed L'kol Chai, Beis Habechirah, R' Chaim Palagi).

10 Siddur Kol Eliyahu

11 Rambam, Hilchos Bikurim, 5:7

change and return.[12]

Another connection of challah to teshuvah is that the process of the mitzvah of challah is three-fold, which connects to the three phases of teshuva as defined by the Baal Shem Tov[13]: submission, separation, and sweetening. Submission is the acknowledgment that the dough, seemingly whole and complete, is imperfect without the removal of a piece. Separation relates to the actual separation of the piece of dough for the mitzvah and the sweetening is the eating and enjoyment of the completed challah.

- The initial shattering in creation occurred from a sense of "I will rule," the serpent's claim that with the eating of the forbidden fruit, Eve and Adam would be like G-d Himself. The rectification of this breaking, the *tikkun* or healing of the world as it were, will come from humility and gratitude, both primary factors in the mitzvah of challah. As such, the separation of challah is a segulah for the healing of our emotional sefirot and, indeed, a healing for the original shattering of the first human, Adam, who was called *"challato shel olam/* the challah of the world" *(Bereishit Rabbah 14:1).*

---

12 *In Challah 2:1 it says that we learn this from the word "shamah/there" in Bamidbar, 15:18: "Speak to the children of Israel and you shall say to them, 'When you arrive in the Land to which I am bringing you shamah/there.'"*

13 *Rabbi Yisrael ben Eliezer, known as the Baal Shem Tov, (d.1760), is the founder of the Chasidic movement.*

Chapter IX
Challah Meditations

Forming the Dough
: MEDITATIONS ON THE INGREDIENTS

Challah is not just a recipe for bread; it is intrinsically a recipe for life itself. Each of the five primary ingredients reflects an essential aspect of life and the nurturing of it.

As we add each ingredient, we become present to the deeper significance of that particular element and allow ourselves to be fully and joyfully in the moment. The challah dough that results is a direct reflection of our intention.

WATER

In the beginning, there was only water. All life emerged from water, water flows from Eden into the world, water breaks and we emerge.

Water, as a primordial element and a life-giving force that continually flows from higher ground to lower places, represents the very essence of life – that part of us that is eternally linked to the Source of all life, namely, our soul.

As we begin the creation of the dough with the pouring of water, we remember that the essence of who we are, and the essential core of those we love, is a precious fragment of the Divine. We, and all of humanity and creation, in fact, are a direct reflection of G-dliness and, as such, we are pure light and goodness at our core. This reminds us of our own inherent worthiness and the innate beauty of those we care for. We begin nurturing with the realization of all of creation's innate holiness and value.

YEAST

We sprinkle in the yeast and reflect upon the fact that this is the ingredient that inflates the challah. This represents the self-esteem, confidence, and reassurance we can give in abundance to those whose lives we directly influence. We can even continually grant small measures of it to each person whose path we cross during our lifetime. The balance of the yeast is crucial to the growth of the dough; we are aiming for a healthy and perfect rising.

SUGAR

Sugar is about creating a sweet environment. While adding sugar, we think about how we can continue injecting chesed, kindness, and sweetness into our home in a way that encourages growth and movement. Sweetness is essential in the beginning of life and throughout life, in fact, and should be used in abundance. That said, just as sugar causes the yeast to activate when used in the right proportions, the tendency of sugar is also to create an overgrowth if applied without restraint or boundaries. And that is where the salt, or gevurah, comes into play. *More on that soon . . . .*

FLOUR

Flour is the main substantial ingredient of bread, which is known as the "staff of life." It represents the physical body and health of our family and of humanity. We need to ensure that our physical vessel is being properly cared for so that we can access our higher self. *"[I]m ein kemach, ein Torah/*[W]ithout flour there is no Torah." When pouring the flour, we meditate on the physical health of those in our care, and pray for their well-being and for the healing of all of humanity.

SALT

Now we can measure in the salt. Salt represents gevurah, boundaries and discipline. When added in correct proportion, salt provides necessary structure to the dough and highlights the sweetness of the challah. Too much salt, however, is harsh and destructive. As we add in the carefully measured amount of salt, we meditate on our gevurah approach with our family and all those we come in contact with. Remember that we add the salt only once the sugar has done its work! Sweetness before harshness always, and always a higher proportion of sugar to salt.

EGGS and OIL

Eggs are a binding ingredient. Conversely, oil is an element that stands apart.

When opening and adding the eggs, we reflect on the elements of similarity that connect us with our families and the numerous factors that remind us of our overall shared humanity. In this way, we draw together and feel accepted, loved, and connected.

While pouring in the oil, we notice how the substance stubbornly resists the melding process, and remember that those things that make us stand apart are the very same qualities that make us singular and valuable. In all the ways our loved ones are different from us and each other, they are unique and chosen. We meditate on the oil and remember to cherish the unique qualities of the ones we love that brighten the world.

VANILLA

This intention is for any added ingredient that we put into our challah just because we like it. When we sprinkle in the flavor of our choice—sweet, savory, or otherwise—we consider the ways in which we nurture that are singular to our personality and life experience. We remember that the best nourishment is the one that comes from an open, honest, and giving place, and we strengthen our resolve to continue nurturing from that place within ourselves.

Meditation While Mixing

The work we do as nurturers, often physical and at times monotonous, is really so much more than meets the eye. In the work we do with our hands, we have the power to inject love and kindness into the hearts of our family and all those around us.

Nurturing and bringing to life is an innately feminine trait that stems from the quality of malchut. As receivers, we are constantly downloading energy and have it within us to transform and infuse those energies into life-giving ingredients, bringing them together to sustain and elevate the lives of those we love.

The act of taking challah is, in and of itself, a great mitzvah. It is a declaration of trust in the sustenance of Hashem and the belief that all we have and all that we are is, in actuality, a direct manifestation of Divine. By extension, the entire process of baking challah becomes an experience of connectivity to G-d and to all of humanity.

Bread is the very essence of sustenance. By baking bread, we are offering life and health to those we love. By putting our devotion and mindfulness into the dough, we are offering spiritual and emotional sustenance, as well.

We remember to remain connected and present during the process, appreciating the fact that by bringing all of ourselves into this moment, we are giving the very best of who we are to the ones who need it the most.

Kneading Meditation I
: TESHUVAH MEDITATION
Hachna'ah, Havdalah & Hamtakah / Submission, Separation & Sweetening

This is an especially appropriate meditation for the months of Elul and Tishrei, and particularly during the 10 days between Rosh Hashanah and Yom Kippur, known as the Aseret Y'mei Teshuvah/ the Ten Days of Repentance. If a woman doesn't usually bake challah, it is recommended that she at least bake (and separate) challah once a year, during these 10 days. This meditation focuses on teshuvah, the process of return, adapted from the teachings of the Baal Shem Tov.

While kneading the dough, we visualize the separate cells of the flour merging with the unifying chesed of water and becoming a more perfect substance than before.

1. *Hachna'ah*/Submission: We bring to mind those things in our own life that bring feelings of regret and brokenness. We allow ourselves to simply be in that reality. Perhaps it is a relationship that has brought pain or separation into our life. Perhaps it is a tragic occurrence that is causing us to feel broken and low, or, perhaps it is simply the pain of feeling disjointed and alienated.

See how the ingredients are messy, scattered all over the bowl (and maybe the kitchen!) and seemingly not the perfect round challah dough that you are dreaming of. Allow that to be the reality for the moment.

2. *Havdalah*/Separation: A great practice when kneading is to walk away from the bowl for a few minutes after the initial mixing. It's good to allow the ingredients to come together on their own somewhat; the gluten starts developing, softening the dough and making the kneading process easier. Additionally, this becomes a part of our three part teshuvah meditation. This is the havdalah/separation stage of healing. In the first stage of submission we reflect on those things that are causing us to feel pain or brokenness in our lives. Now, we walk away from these issues and observe them from a distance, realizing that they are not part of our essential self. They are external garments to our self, not an appendage that is permanently attached to, or defining, us.

3. *Hamtakah*/Sweetening: Now we return to our kneading job.

As we scrape together all the bits and pieces of flour and other various scattered ingredients and incorporate them into the perfection of our dough, we knead these hurts back into our life. This time, however, we see them clearly for what they are. Not our defining traits, they are separate to our essential wholeness. In reintegrating the mistakes or the wrongs that were done by us or to us, we see how they all come together to form a perfect roundness. Everything becomes part of the circle of our life and our existence. This is the sweetening, the healing of our story. The sweetening continues with the final blessing and eating of the baked challah, when we truly integrate the challah, and all of the once disparate particles, into ourselves and allow it to become part of our beautiful future.

Kneading Meditation II

: "Ein od Milvado / There is nothing else besides the oneness of Hashem"

When kneading all the ingredients together, we meditate on the unification of all of creation. We observe how all things that seem separate to us in our lives—be it people, events, even our own emotions and reactions—are really one, an inextricable part of G-d, the Source of all creation and sustenance.

"The earth will be filled with the intimate knowledge of Hashem, as the waters fill the seas" (Yeshayahu 11:9). As the water brings all ingredients together and reveals their inherent unity, so, too, the knowledge of the single Source of all of creation and the intimate oneness of all existence fills our frame of awareness and awakens us to *"ein od milvado/* there is nothing besides Him."

By recognizing the oneness of all creation and the infinite potentiality of blessing that a state of unity brings, we draw down tremendous blessing into our challah, our homes, and our lives.

Hafrashat Challah
: MEDITATION FOR SEPARATING THE CHALLAH

As we lay our hands upon the dough to recite the blessing, we allow all of time to pause for a moment. All the hustle and bustle of preparing the dough, the frenetic activity of Shabbat preparation—it all dissolves in this span of silence. This is not a time for active engagement, it is a time for deep contemplation and processing.

The feel of the dough beneath our hands is warm and alive. We have put the best of ourselves into the making of this. Our weeklong efforts to secure financial sustenance have allowed us to buy and collect the necessary ingredients and the work of our hands has kneaded it together and formed this perfect dough that we now rest our weary hands upon. At this moment it is easy to feel a niggling of pride and vanity: *"The strength and power of my own two hands have made this happen for me" (Devarim 8:17).*

However, as we prepare the challah we are moving from the weekday reality of feeling our own creativity powering our success, to the Shabbat reality of recognizing that all that sustains us is sourced in the One above. When we remove a piece of dough, the "challah gift," we are acknowledging the deep truth that all that we have and all that we have done, is by the grace of G-d. The world and all that is in it belongs to Hashem and we are but grateful partakers of His goodness.

If we were merely physical beings, collections of atoms and particles, we would be limited to material reality. We would essentially be prisoners of physical matter, chained to cause and effect. But we are not physical creatures. We are a soul, enclothed in the garb of flesh and blood. We are not entrapped by the laws of physics and not bound by the dictates of science.

"He breathed into his nostrils the neshamah of life" (Bereishit 2:7). As the Alter Rebbe explains it in Tanya, this means that we are truly and completely a part of the Divine that enlivens each one of us at all moments. This is to say that at our very core we are a G-dly breath, a deep and essential Divine element that transcends and gives life to all physical matter.

The taking of the piece of challah is our reminder of this essential truth. If we were but a creature of matter, our deepest concern would be that of our physical survival. The ego would rule and it would be an "each man for himself" reality. If we can remove a piece of our sustenance and declare it to be sourced in a higher origin, we are then connecting to that nucleus of our self that is sourced in the fountainhead of G-dliness.

Recite the blessing and feel the energy flow downwards, beginning in the Source of all brachot/blessings – that endless reservoir of all goodness and light – and culminating in the blessing within the dough beneath your palms.

Tear off a small piece of the dough. Feel the ripping of one reality into the next. This is the tearing off of our smallness, our attachment to this physical world, and the release into the world of formless and infinite possibility.

After separating the dough, hold it for a moment in your hand as you declare it to be challah. "Harei zu challah." This small chunk of dough is a portion of your sustenance that you are willingly and joyfully relinquishing. This is the truest sense of tzedakah/justice. When the dough was given to the priest in the Temple, it was the highest form of giving that was possible. To give of our sustenance is to relinquish our ego, our very survival instinct, to go beyond our humanity, and become G-dlike in that moment.

When we hold the challah in our hand, we are, for that moment, transcending our physical restrictions and limitations and the time/space/cause/effect continuum of the physical world and entering a place of infinity.

In this space all is still formless and possible—and it is from this place that we pray for all blessings to be revealed.

Meditation While Eating the Challah

"You shall serve Hashem your G-d and He will bless your bread and your water . . ." (Shemot 23:25).

The Baal Shem Tov explains this to mean that when we speak words of Torah during our meals, the words become the soul for the physicality [of the food] that is on the table. While eating the challah, we meditate upon the fact that the Creator's presence resides within His food. As we ingest and digest this challah, we are conscious of Hashem's blessing enlivening us and giving us energy, both physical and spiritual, through the absorption of the challah.

The above verse in *Shemot* continues by saying, *"and I will remove all sickness from your midst."* As we partake of the challah, we meditate on the spiritual healing properties of the challah and have the intention that the blessing in this challah will serve to eradicate all illness from our lives and bring perfect wholeness and health.

RISING

"YOU CAN STAND AND LOOK AT THEM, EVEN THE FIRST TIME, WITH AN ALMOST MYSTICAL PRIDE AND FEELING OF SELF-PLEASURE. YOU WILL KNOW, AS YOU SMELL THEM AND REMEMBER THE STRANGE COOL SOLIDITY OF THE DOUGH PUFFING UP AROUND YOUR WRIST WHEN YOU HIT IT, WHAT PEOPLE HAVE KNOWN FOR CENTURIES ABOUT THE SANCTITY OF BREAD. YOU WILL UNDERSTAND WHY CERTAIN SIMPLE MEN, IN OLD CENTURIES, USED TO APOLOGIZE TO THE FAMILY LOAF IF BY ACCIDENT THEY DROPPED IT FROM THE TABLE."

— MFK FISHER, HOW TO COOK A WOLF

SECTION II:

Making the Challah
GROUNDING INTENTION IN PRACTICE

RISING

It's been great sharing with you about the deeper significance of challah and how every aspect of the making of it mirrors our nurturing potential. But I think it's time we actually got our hands in a bowl and made some challah!

This section of the book, *Making the Challah*, is where the lofty becomes alive and we get to partake of the fruits of our labors.

I have kept it simple in this volume, sharing with you exactly what you will need to make a fantastic, no-fail challah using my "Classic Challah Recipe" and thorough directions, including illustrated instructions for shaping a six-braided challah.

However, please note that the following pages are but a small taste of the offerings in my challah cookbook entitled *RISING! The Book of Challah.*

In the *RISING* cookbook there will be an entire cookbook's worth of drool-worthy challah recipes, including healthful options such as spelt, whole wheat, sourdough, and gluten-free, as well as many creative twists on the traditional challah recipe and even recipes for using leftover challah and extra dough!

Also included in the *RISING* cookbook is a thorough exploration of the challah making process, including a digest of all ingredients, and variations/substitutions for the basic ingredients, and handy and helpful charts to illuminate the challah making process like never before!

Kneading and rising techniques, baking, freezing, and storing are also all address thoroughly. It's like having a challah baking expert hold your hand through the process! I hope you will buy the larger volume and enjoy all it has to offer! From my kitchen, to yours. . . with love.

(See page 184 for a preview of Section II's offerings in RISING! The Book of Challah.)

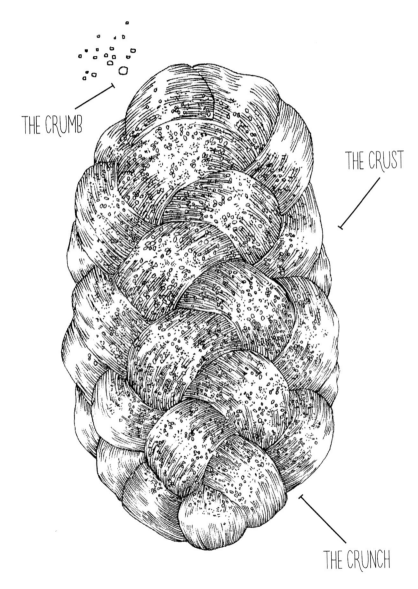

THE CRUMB

THE CRUST

THE CRUNCH

Anatomy of a "Perfect Challah"

The Perfect Challah is crisp with various shades of golden on the outside and a little "something, something" that crunches in your mouth at its very top. Cut through its snappy crust to its innards and it is moist yet somehow still airy, with a delicate, rich crumb (that's breadspeak for the yummy inside of bread!). It is more dense than a regular bread, a close relative to the pound cake, and only a dubious acquaintance of a New York rye.

(A note to my dear, diverse readers: there are those who prefer their challah to be more breadlike with an open and airy crumb. I have just the recipe for you. But, you will have to humor my love of vanilla and dense, rich challah until we get to it. If you absolutely can't bear the wait, *run*, and buy a copy of RISING!, my challah cookbook.)

Ok, so here's my caveat for this chapter, "Anatomy of a Perfect Challah," which you will notice, I have surrounded in quotation marks.

When challah is homemade, it may be perfect in its love, intention, and offering. *This does not mean that it will look perfect.* Every single week it will be slightly different. Sometimes it may look downright frightening. Although allow me to say – beauty is indeed in the eyes of the beholder – I personally have never seen an ugly challah.

This is the beauty of the homemade Challah. If you want uniformity, symmetry, and general blandness, look no further than your local bakery!

Homemade Challah is a reflection of your current state of mind and heart and is not meant to look bakery made—it's meant to look like you made it by yourself! *(Yes, think 3rd grade messy art project.)*

I have been kneading, rising, braiding, and baking for close to 20 years now and my challahs are still not flawless in their appearance. But they are delicious. And lumpy, crooked, or weird as they may sometimes be, my children will not touch "bakery challah." I am happy to say I have spoiled them to delicious imperfection.

It's not about the final result; the process is where it's at.

I'm going to share with you a recipe you won't find anywhere else. I know. I've looked. It took me many years to find/create the perfect challah recipe.

This recipe is built upon countless other recipes that I have worked with in the past, most of them quite good, though none of them as completely amazing as this one! The thing with this recipe is . . . IT'S NO FAIL. Yes, I'm talking to you, Miss I-Give-Duncan-Hines a-Bad-Name.

Over my many years of teaching challah classes, I have seen countless women succeed beyond their happiest imaginings to create a challah they were proud to serve. Many of these women had previously tried baking challah and failed in epic ways. Have you ever met someone with challah PTSD? I think I may actually have seen this in its severe form!

But, after talking through the challah making process and breaking it down, with this recipe in hand, I have seen this trauma completely transformed.

Women all over are baking challah with this incredible recipe and they are thrilled with the results, although, I would venture to say, the people lucky enough to taste it are even more so.

Enough chatting, let's make some challah!

Rebbetzin Rochie's Classic Challah

This is as close to a perfect challah as you can get, IMHO. Moist, sweet, and super light on the inside with a beautiful crust on the outside, the best part of this recipe is that it is NO FAIL. Ever. Everyone who has ever tried this recipe has been thrilled with the results. Are you ready to bake an incredible challah? Here goes!

Note: this recipe can be made with spelt flour or whole wheat with only slight variations. For a spelt challah; add 3 eggs to the recipe, bringing the total eggs to 5 (not including the glaze). For a whole wheat challah, replace all or half the flour with whole wheat and double the rising time.

RECIPE SIZES & YIELDS

1. FULL RECIPE

Yield: 8 1lb challahs

Each 1lb challah yields
6 small challah rolls
or 3 large rolls

Challah should be separated with a blessing when making this proportion of dough. Please see page 129 for detailed instructions.

2. HALF RECIPE

Yield: 4 1lb challahs

Challah should be separated without a blessing when making this proportion of dough. Please see the Digest of Laws of Hafrashat Challah on page 128 for complete instructions.

3. QUARTER RECIPE

Yield: 2 1lb challahs

No challah separation or blessing with this amount of dough.

CHALLAH RECIPE

Ingredients according to recipe size
(Instructions on following page)

FULL	HALF	QUARTER		
4$^{3/4}$	2	1	cup	**WARM WATER** baby-bath temperature, almost hot
1$^{1/2}$	3/4	1/4	cup	**SUGAR** or HONEY
7	5	2$^{1/4}$	tsp	**GRANULATED YEAST**
6	4	2	cup	white, all purpose, unbleached **FLOUR**
2$^{1/2}$	1$^{1/2}$	2/3	Tbsp	**SEA SALT**
1	1/2	1/8	cup	**CANOLA OIL**
2	1/2	1/4	tsp	**VANILLA EXTRACT**
2	2	1+yolk	large	**EGGS**
7-9	2-3.5	1-1.25	cup	**FLOUR**

CHALLAH GLAZE

1 egg, well beaten with 1 tsp. water

(OPTIONAL) CHALLAH TOPPINGS
Use one or use them all!

poppy seeds / sesame seeds /
coarse sea salt / sugar / honey

RISING

STEP BY STEP INSTRUCTIONS

A note before getting started.

The first step is proofing the yeast, which simply means ensuring that the yeast is alive and activating it. This is done by dissolving the yeast in very warm water, which I like to qualify as "baby bathwater." It should not be hot. Some sugar is also added to the water, assisting in the activation of the yeast. If using dry, instant yeast there is no need to wait for the yeast to begin foaming. If using fresh yeast, allow approximately 10 minutes for the yeast to activate in the water and sugar before moving on to step 2. You will know that the yeast is active when you see bubbles, or foamy blobs, rising to the surface of the water. After 10 minutes or so, the entire surface should almost be covered with a foamy froth.

Step 1. In a large challah bowl, pour very warm **WATER**. Add the **YEAST** and **SUGAR**. Allow a few minutes for frothing. (see note above)

Step 2. Add the *first* **FLOUR** measurement and the **SALT** and mix until you have a smooth batter.

Step 3. Add **EGGS, OIL**, and **VANILLA** and stir again until smooth.

Step 4. Add the rest of the **FLOUR**, eventually working the dough with your hands (or, if using a mixer, adding the dough hook attachment now). Add the rest of the flour *gradually*, being sure not to add too much, until the dough is workable and lifts away from the sides of the bowl.

Step 5. **Knead** for about 7-10 minutes, or until the dough springs back when lightly touched.

Step 6. Pour or spray a little oil (a teaspoon or two) in a large bowl (you can use the same bowl in which you made the dough). Turn the ball of dough in the oil, coating the outer layer of the dough.

Step 7. **Cover the bowl** with plastic wrap or a warm, damp dishcloth. Put in a warm spot to rise.

Step 8. **Allow to rise** for 1.5-2.5 hours (depending on the temperature in your home). If allowing to rise for longer, be sure to punch out some air sometime during the rising.

Step 9. **Separate the dough** if necessary, with or without a blessing, depending on the size of your dough. *See page 134 for blessing.*

Step 10. Preheat the oven to **350°F**.

Step 11. Divide the dough into two, four or eight equal pieces, (depending on the size dough you are making) each one of these pieces will make approximately a 1lb challah. Begin shaping or **braiding**. *See page 178 for braiding instructions.*

Step 12. Brush each challah with the **EGG GLAZE** immediately after braiding.

Step 13. Allow the shaped challahs to **rise** for another 30 – 45 minutes.

Step 14. Very gently glaze once again and sprinkle on topping of choice.

Step 15. **Bake** at 350°F. A 1 lb challah will bake in approximately 30 minutes. Allow more time for larger challahs and less for smaller ones.

Step 16. Remove from oven when top is golden brown and bottom is crisp and sounds hollow when tapped. Place on cooling rack to cool off.

STORING AND FREEZING YOUR CHALLAH

STORING CHALLAH

To store your challahs, keep in plastic bags such as Ziploc bags, that are tightly sealed. They should keep well for about 2-3 days.

FREEZING CHALLAH

If you plan to serve the challahs more than a day or two after baking, I highly recommend freezing either the unbaked, braided loaves or the fully baked challahs.

CHALLAH INSTRUCTIONS

Freezing unbaked challah

Allow the dough to rise, punch down, separate the challah and make the blessing. You can then braid the challah, brush a light coat of oil over the loaf, and place it immediately in a tightly sealed bag in the freezer.

To bake the frozen challah, remove it from the bag and allow it to fully defrost (time for this will depend on the size of the challah, but approximately 3-6 hours)

Glaze the challah and allow to rise again. Glaze once more, add toppings, and bake as usual.

Freezing baked challah

Allow the baked challah to cool completely on the cooling rack. This may even mean a few hours of cooling.

Place in tightly sealed plastic bag and place in freezer.

A 1 lb challah will defrost in about 2 hours and small rolls in about an hour or less.

When defrosted, place in preheated oven at 350°F for 8-10 minutes, they will taste just-baked!

Braiding a Beautiful Challah

In this volume I will be demonstrating the technique for a gorgeous six-braid challah. While the instructions may look complex, you will see that once you get the hang of it, it's really not hard at all! Keep at it, your first attempts may not be perfect, but eventually you will master it and the results will be well worth the effort!

I will also show you the simple challah knot roll (also known as challah buns or bulkelach, which is what we called them as children.)

A beautiful challah begins with lovely strands. I will give you some technique for this as well, to help you acheive your beauty of a challah.

For a tremendous variety of braiding technique, see my cookbook RISING! The Book of Challah. Preview on pages 183-186

ROLLING OUT THE STRANDS

To achieve a challah with that is nicely tapered at the ends and full and high in the center it helps to start with a strand that is tapered.

There are two methods of rolling out the strands. Either way, start with a small rounded piece of dough. To create a 1 lb challah, each of the six pieces should weigh approx 2.67 oz. If you have a kitchen scale, go ahead and plop the dough pieces on there. At least until you get a feel for the size.

Sprinkle a little bit of flour on your working surface so the dough doesn't stick. *Now let's get started!*

1. Rolling out a strand: the quick way!

[a] Using the palm of your hands, start rolling out the dough, first with your stronger hand and then as it lengthens, add your second hand. Work towards the outer edges of the strand, applying more pressure as you get closer to the ends. This will give your strands a nice, tapered shape. *Be sure not to flatten the strands, we are going for logs, not 2x4 planks!*

2. Rolling out a strand: the fancier way!

This method is not that much more time consuming than the first, and the advantage is that you end up with beautifully smooth strands, without any of the bumpiness you might see with the other method.

This method also introduces more air into each strand, creating a slightly airier loaf.

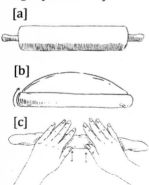

[a] Make sure your working surface is floured. Using a rolling pin, flatten out the ball of dough, rolling the pin away from you. Don't worry too much about the shape you're creating.

[b] Roll the flattened dough into a strand. [c] Gently roll the completed strand to close up the seam and pushing outwards, taper the ends.

BRAIDING A CHALLAH: SIX-STRANDS

There are different methods of braiding with six strands, however this particular technique results in a beautifully high and zaftig challah. Just the way I like it!

I. Begin with 6 even strands. *See previous page for strand rolling techniques.*

2. Pinch the very tops of the strands together. Try not to create a big lump of dough at the top. The tops of the strands should just be lightly pressed together.

3. *We will now create our "X" formation that we'll be keeping througout the braiding process.*
Begin by lifting #2 and crossing over to the top right. Then take #6 and crossing over strand 2, place it on the top left.

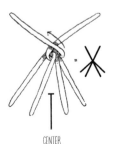

Now you have somewhat of an "X" formation. Keep this formation throughout the braiding.

Always make sure you are clear where the center is, between the four bottom strands. You will always be bringing the top strands into the center.

Now we begin working from side to side.

180

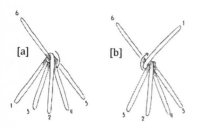

4. Begin with the right, [a] bring strand #2 back down, into the center. [b] Bring strand #1 from the left up to replace it.

Now re-orient yourself with the bottom strands making sure you can clearly see the center. Keep re-orienting after each down, up sequence.

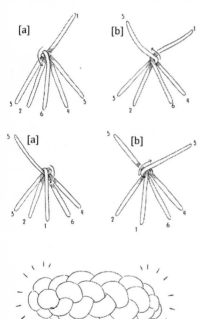

5. Working from the left side now, [a] bring strand #6 back down into the center and [b] bring #5 from the right up to replace it.

6. Back to the right side now, [a] bring strand #1 back down into the center and [b] bring #3 from the left up to replace it.

7. Back to the left side side now, bring strand #5 back down into the center and continue with the down from one side and up from the other until you've reached the end of the strands.

Don't worry if the strands don't all end at the same time, when you can't braid anymore, just gather all the bits of remaining strands, pinch them together and tuck tightly under the challah. Voilà! It's a challah!

SHAPING A CHALLAH ROLL: THE "BULKELAH"

This is a super quick way to make little individual challah buns.

1. Begin with 1 strand. Cross over, leaving a space to pull the end through.

2. Bring the strand up and through the hole. You will have one end sticking out on top and one on the bottom of the challah roll.

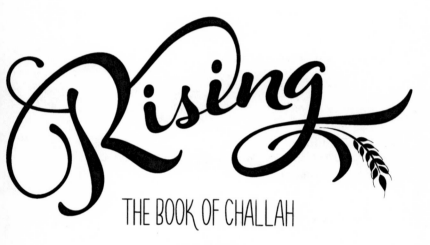

THE BOOK OF CHALLAH

ROCHIE PINSON

THE CHALLAH COOKBOOK
FELDHEIM PUBLISHERS 2015

A taste of what's to come in *RISING! The Book of Challah.*

RISING! The Book of Challah is a challah cookbook as you have never seen it! Besides for including all of the material in Section I of this book, here is a sneak peek into the offerings you'll find.

1. Preparing to Bake a Challah

The Ingredients
A thorough exploration and explanation of the ingredients you will need for baking a challah. Included is a list of recommended ingredients and specialty items.

The Equipment
All the tips and tricks for what you'll need on hand to bake the most beautiful challah.

2. Making a Challah

The Basic Steps and Technique for Making Any Challah

Kneading Techniques

Rising Techniques

Storing and Freezing

Troubleshooting a Troublesome Dough

3. Recipes

A treasurehouse of the most incredible challah recipes, *RISING!* includes:

Rebbetzin Rochie's Classic Challah
Whole Wheat Honey Challah
White Whole Wheat Challah

Gluten-Free Challah
Vegan Challah
Spelt Challah
Sourdough Challah

Holiday/Specialty Challahs
Pumpkin Challah
Apple Honey Challah
Pretzel Challah
Olive Oil, Kalamata, and Rosemary Challah
Shivat Minim Challah
Shavuot Butter Challah Two Ways: Sweet & Savory

Exotic Challahs
Sephardic Challah
Moroccan Challah
Yemenite Lachuch / Flat Challah Bread
Yemenite Kubaneh / Shabbat Breakfast Bread
Bukharian Leposhka

Leftover Challah Recipes
Chocolate Pull Apart Babka
Cinnamon Rolls with Cream Cheese frosting
Cheddar Spinach Strata
Challah, Wild Mushroom & Herb Stuffing
Garlic Croutons
Lemon Vanilla French Toast

4. Braiding and Shaping the Challah

Beautifully photographed and illustrated, easiest instructions to follow. You'll be wowing them with your flawless challahs in no time!

Braiding Techniques

3,4,6 & 8 Braid Techniques

Challah rolls 3 ways

Holiday Specialty Shapes

Post Pesach: Schlissel Challah

Sukkot: Lulav and Esrog Challah

Purim: Hamentash Challah

Rosh Hashana: Round Braided and Round Turban

Tu B'Shvat: Grape Challah

Shavuot: Floral Wreath Challah

ABOUT THE AUTHOR

Rochie Pinson is a mother, artist, and rebbetzin of a large and growing community in Brownstone Brooklyn. Rochie is a Chabad emissary and the co-founder of the IYYUN Center for Jewish Spirituality which reaches thousands of people every year, both locally and globally, with classes, events, social media and a website, and the publication of many books devoted to Judaism and spirituality.

In her capacity as rebbetzin, Rochie is a mentor to hundreds of women in her community and beyond. She also lectures and leads seminars around the world.

Rebbetzin Rochie has a unique blend of wisdom, spiritual awareness, and down-to-earth practicality. Her voice is both humorous and wise and appeals to a wide audience. You can follow her through her web journal at **therisinglife.net.**

CPSIA information can be obtained
at www.ICGtesting.com
Printed in the USA
FFOW02n1943150715
15230FF

9 780989 007245